DRE WILLIAMS

IT'S ALREADY DONE

A POWERFUL STORY
OF DELIVERANCE AND TRANSFORMATION

It's Already Done:
A Powerful Story of Deliverance and Transformation.

by Dre Williams

copyright ©2019 DeAndre Williams

ISBN: 978-1-950718-15-3

published by Kudu Publishing
cover design by Kiryl Lysenka

It's Already Done is available in Amazon Kindle, Barnes & Noble Nook and Apple iBooks.

CONTENTS

FOREWORD

SPEAKING SELFISHLY, THIS moment is a long-awaited one. I believe this book will be a blessing for decades to come. If I can imagine Dre as a little child, he would have been an intellectual little being with an extensive vocabulary beyond his years—not just big words, but words that hold so much wisdom. Great wisdom would come from that little one. I imagine his mind working overtime, so much so that his adversary would have a glimpse of what "Little Dre" would become in later years.

Through tough times, heartaches, loneliness, and abandonment, he has fought. He fights, he loves, and he cares. He gives what he's never had. And I think people with similar stories and backgrounds are also perfect fighters, lovers, and caregivers. You may be the same. Not giving up. Simply wanting to make an impact on this world. Knowing deep down inside that you didn't go through all of that for nothing. As you read *It's Already Done*—the very first of many books by Dre—you'll certainly be encouraged. It is a powerful story of deliverance, and I pray you are blessed as you read. I'm happy to call him my hubby.

—Llechor

INTRODUCTION

Y NAME IS DEANDRE CARTEZ WILLIAMS. You can call me "Dre." I feel the proper way of introducing myself is sticking to what I know—myself. Thank you for taking time out of your life to look through my eyes for a moment. I appreciate you so very much!

I wrote this book so you could get to know this weak and foolish vessel used by the Master to accomplish great things. I have dealt with many difficult challenges in my 41 years of life, and I want you to know some of them. I have also experienced many good things as well. As you read through these pages, you will laugh, cry, and be inspired to know God in greater detail. You will also be encouraged to be a better version of yourself. You will feel my passion for teaching as well. So be prepared to learn!

This is my first book. I am taking you back to where it all started, before I learned of my talents in music, writing, speaking, and leadership—long before I stepped on stages to preach and teach God's Word. This book is real and raw, detailing my story and struggle. I'm a fighter by nature, and I do not like to lose.

I have observed winners for years through watching their resolve in conflict. I wanted the same for my life. Some of my hardships, which you will read about in this book, will shock you and make you appreciate your life more. This book will bless and inspire you to get closer to God. I am an underdog in every sense of the word, the least likely to succeed, but one who found his voice and freedom. This book is for the underdog as well as the favorite. This book will make you reconsider your outlook on life. It will rekindle your passion and determination to face the giants of life with courage.

It has taken me until now to see that God has already predestined each of us to triumph in this life. Our triumphant journeys will be interrupted by enemies, opponents, and failures. So, stop worrying and move forward! This book will convince you that it's already done!

chapter 1

WHAT GOD?!...BUT GOD!

"Why, Lord, do you stand far off? Why do you hide yourself in times of trouble?" —Psalms 10:1

I WAS BORN AUGUST 7, 1978, in St. Louis, Missouri. Barnes Hospital did not have a clue it would host the greatest athlete of his era! Well, maybe I'm not the world's greatest athlete, and maybe I'm not the greatest of anything. However, I would say that my existence was unexpected and heartbreaking. My mom was 16 years old when she had me. My dad was 19. He loved his share of women, and my parents never married. I'm pretty sure both never wanted such a responsibility at that irresponsible stage of their lives.

I am the father of two beautiful daughters. Their names are DeYanni and Lauren. I had my first, rather my wife

Llechor gave birth to our first, when I was 26 years old. My grandfather was in his early 40's just as I am now–when my mother gave birth to me. I cannot imagine one of my babies getting pregnant at age anything-before-50! I have often wondered what my grandfather felt when he was told the news. I heard he cried, but I never spoke with him about it. I would ask, but I do not want him to feel any pain again, even if it is ever so slight, these days.

With tears in my mother's eyes coupled with screams of pain, out came little DeAndre. She gave me her maiden name Williams due to things not working out between her and my father. I don't knock them for their teenage breakup. How many of those relationships work out? I did resent the absence of my father's presence in my life. His missing spirit left me confused growing up. We moved around a lot, and I witnessed my mother struggle to make ends meet. Some years we couldn't even find the ends!

As a child in the front-row seat of her life, I watched my mother frantically rally our home. She suffered from drug abuse, bad boyfriends who got physical, and lack of resources. She always referred to me as the "Man of the House," a title that fit me like an NFL uniform on a Pee Wee Leaguer. It was a burden placed on my young shoulders. My mother didn't know that, but it resided there nonetheless.

My mom, cradling me in her adolescent arms, now faced a dilemma many women in America face: the single-mom life. She scrubbed airplanes in inclement weather, cleaned dirty hotel rooms, argued with losers, and battled addictions that would bind her soul for years. I wrestled with our conditions. They frustrated me. I didn't understand them. They isolated me. They also branded me a statistic and victim. We were broken, a black family in a predominately white society. Our dreams trampled, hope deferred, hearts sick, hands droopy.

My mother would eventually marry, and from that union a beautiful person was born, a kind-hearted, compassionate man who is my brother, Lynn Brown. I loved him like a son; I was very excited (At least I remember it that way!) at his entrance into the world. Those feelings of excitement turned to bitterness as my mom and her husband fell on hard times. He was an animal. I partially blame him for her chemical dependency. I forgive him for it, but he crushed her domestically. I will get into more details of how in later chapters, but I want you to get a sense of what my early childhood entailed.

My lead off Bible text comes from the life of a warrior by the name of David. He was fiercely competitive. He wiped the floor with his enemies. King David as he would later become is repeatedly referred to as "A man after God's own heart" (1 Sam. 13:14). You know the phrase; it is used mostly by worship leaders, preachers, and pastors.

WHAT DOES IT REALLY MEAN?

David was not the first picked; he was one of seven brothers. They did not respect or know what was embedded deeply within him. David did the dirty work of the family defending the sheep of the family business. This lowly job, I am sure, afforded him plenty of opportunities to hear the voice of the Lord. He grew according to the patriarchal standard set by his forefathers.

After hearing about the accomplishments of Jehovah, after viewing his brothers' productivity from afar, he wanted evidence for himself. This longing, this desire for divine affirmation resulted in a man who wanted God's thoughts more than his own. This is what it means when you hear the crowd-pleasing phrase "A man after God's own heart." Our verse strikes a chord in my heart that is off-key. Then I am reminded that life hands out more questions than answers, problems than solutions, and pain than comfort. No matter how multi-talented or gifted I am, there is a hurt part on the inside of me that I swallowed many years ago that has lately been causing me nausea.

It is not every string of my heart that is discordant, just a few that sound worse than a butchered Star-Spangled Banner solo. There are not too many of them, just enough to make me question my purpose at times. Just enough to make me want to throw it all away. Pain produces negativity, and anything sinful left to itself can produce harmful, catastrophic results in anyone's life.

BUT...GOD!

God lifts me out of that dark place of despair and discouragement. He protects my unprotected areas with grace and dignity. I'm reminded often that if it had not been for Jesus, that monstrous stepfather I told you about could have murdered my mom, my little brother, and me. That man's wickedness was held back for a special reason that only heaven knows. If it's already done, meaning my life has been played in symphonic harmony with the Master, by a cluster of circumstances, rhythmically interwoven for good, how could I not be intrigued? You see, I believe my life's events have been divinely arranged.

My early childhood, filled with horrific events that you will read about in this book, serves a purpose to set millions of people in bondage free and makes perfect sense! "What God, But God," will forever remain banded together in my heart because He always works things out for our good (Rom. 8:28)! Every victory we will ever win interconnects with the belief that God is for us! He's already won it all for each person who has lived, now lives, and will ever live. The good has already been done. We must believe it.

You may ask, "Dre, if there is a God and He is real, why does He allow all of these problems in the world? Why is our country so divided? Why are our churches so segregated on Sundays when the Word says to dwell together in unity (Psalms 133:1)? Why are so many school systems broken? Why are American jails more populated than any other country?" And on and on you may question.

What I can tell you is this: But God! It must be applied if we are to look at our suffering society accurately. Without His presence there would be no example of good in the earth. We would have no way of understanding what true happiness is. For every death there's life, for every loss there is something gained. For every frown, a smile. For every defeat there is a victory. If our world was forsaken by God (as if it could ever be), you tell me how survival would survive. I don't agree with all of God's judgments, but I am smart enough to respect them. Life at times makes us say, "What God?" out of pure shock and anger.

People betray us; they lie to us and come with hidden agendas. They envy our work and belittle our efforts. To be frank, some humans wake up with no other intention but to cause harm. To release a stroke of wickedness on the unsuspecting and innocent. Some people are sneaky, conniving, and ruthless. They show no mercy and lie to maintain an advantage. They are vicious and unconscious to love. Puny in confidence, jumbo in insecurity, undesirable of change. Do you know what our Father does at pivotal points in our lives? He drops them dead-center into our world! What? Why? We try with every effort and all the energy we can muster to escape the inevitable hurt that will come our way, to no avail. Does this sound familiar? Are you like one of these people?

If you relate, there is mercy for both the innocent and the guilty. I don't condemn, but I have questioned the wisdom of God many times in my life. The "What God?" moments of some people's lives have destructed beyond repair their ability to understand. Others have transferred that negative mindset onto the next generation, our precious children. I'm not saying they've done it intentionally, yet even if subconsciously communicated, their ideas can leave a lasting impact and legacy. It is hard for me at times to depend on God for long-term good and not settle for instant revenge on my enemies. It takes faith to not ask questions, to just resign oneself to the peace of God.

Here in this text we see David, the great challenger who slew the triumphant Goliath. David told him in advance that the unprecedented would take place. It was David who unflinchingly stood up to the great enemy of Israel who taunted, roasted, and trolled its army. Goliath demanded one of them come out to fight him. It was David who never hesitated to crush the defiant herculean warrior using unconventional tools. It was David who reached a point in his life that made him question the sovereignty of God. How dare he?

How can a man used by God so greatly, many times over, suddenly probe the One who is above all lines of questioning?

STANDOFFISH?

It is one thing to ask, "Why?" I think it is far worse to accuse the omnipotent God of the universe of moving away from His post! It is as if David is saying, "God, You are there during the good times, when the waters are calm, when the clouds are nonthreatening. What about now?" Have you ever felt this way? When the shadows of trouble give chase? Be they bills, job loss, injury or infirmity, our feelings never welcome the adversity that is in hot pursuit of us.

I have met famous people in this life. I find it pleasant to my soul to find them humble and approachable. It annoys me greatly to meet a celebrity who is standoffish, especially if I admire their work. This snobbish aspect of their personality just rubs me the wrong way. This example reminds me of what it may have felt like for David to feel abandoned by his God. I can hear the angst of his heart cry, "I'm after Your heart! I love You! I've served as faithfully as I could. Why?" He was overcome by the success of the wicked. He felt the perceived inactivity of God. David wanted answers.

HIDDEN FIGURE

I want to shed even more light on David's bitter disappointment in God by moving to the next point of his questioning. He asked the Lord why He would "hide" in times of trouble. What a statement! What honesty! Modern Christianity doesn't know how to handle scriptures like this. We portray God as Santa who rewards the naughty and nice equally, a genie who when rubbed rightly, pops out instantly, granting all wishes! Our generation teaches a socially friendly Jesus who comes when He's wanted and is always on time.

The saints of old had a saying: He may not come when you want Him, but He's always right on time! He's there before the child gets molested. He's there before the car accident. He's there before divorce papers are signed. He's there before our votes are cast. I hate to disappoint anyone who believes that old saying, but it is simply not true. This text proves it. Sometimes God chooses to not move when we feel it is most necessary. Many times He makes us wait, and wait, and wait some more, and when we get tired of waiting, wait even longer! As painful and unscriptural as it feels, I believe God is there! He may decide to give strength instead of removing the issue. I may have to press in, but I'll touch the hem!

We love the story of the issue of blood; it's a staple in the minds of faithful churchgoers. In Matthew 9:20–22, we have a desperate, despised woman determined to get to Jesus. The crowds often pressed Jesus everywhere He frequented because as Tasha Cobbs sang so emphatically, "I want to be where You are. I got to be where You are!" We hail this woman a heroine due to her persistence. She refused to go back home leaking; "No" was not an option. She caught just a cramped flash of the Son of God and felt it was all she needed to begin her press. Jesus, swarmed by the crowd like a hidden figure. One woman touched only the fringe of His raiment! She had waited 12 years! She'd bled for 4,380 days. How many wraps and layers? How many attempts to discover a remedy? How many laughs from mockers? How many nights of restless sleep? When we are forced to wait, it makes us despair. We grit our teeth. We clench our fists. It hardens us with its capacity to make us weary.

BUT GOD!

This persevering princess said, "No more!" She forced her way to get what her soul needed. Total deliverance! David eventually experienced brighter days. He moved past his place of bitterness to see the sweet mercy and compassion of Jehovah God who wishes no man would perish, but that all would come to repentance (2 Pet. 3:9).

Faced with my own moments of bitterness and anger, I had to accept the silence and privacy of God. Those years were horrible! The delayed gratification, the painful weight of trouble most days was too much to bear. Yet now many years later, I am learning to see my birth as a blessing instead of a blemish. As a child I believed I had ruined the hopes and dreams of my juvenile mother. I felt my life limited her pay bracket; I also believed I kept her from years of exploration.

Yet now, due to all I have endured, I live to share with you! This gives me a sense of peace and purpose, as well as confidence. I believe that my life has already been played out, predetermined by the hand of God. Nothing could ever convince me otherwise for all eternity. When it comes to the shaping and detailing of our lives, we may not understand it all or even care to look back. But I can assure you of this: It's already done!

chapter 2

THE IMMACULATE ACCIDENT

"I praise you because I am fearfully and wonderfully made. Your works are wonderful; I know that full well." —Psalms 139:14

"**T**HERE ARE NO MISTAKES, only happy accidents," said the afro-wearing, iconic artisan Bob Ross. I like his sentiment; it is insightful and uplifting. Mr. Ross is one of my favorite artists. His world-renowned painting style took the world by the hand in the early 80s to mid 90s and gently danced with it until the day he was called home in 1995. America and the world mourned the loss of an incredibly gifted, gentle soul. Bob made a living out of "accidents."

He tossed out the intrinsic eye of perfection, and created an instrumental to the accidental. His soundtrack is still set to repeat in the hearts of those who love both him and his work.

I can't help but wonder if this beautifully painted, metaphorical statement could truly be sketched in our hearts today. Could it truly be possible that children born out of wedlock to unsuspecting parents have purpose? What good comes from a miscarriage? We know that Isaac was blessed, but what about us "Ishmaels?" Could those whose birth wasn't right have a right of birth? These are the sorts of questions we all ponder from time to time. They press us; they are conundrums.

Conundrum: a riddle, anything that puzzles

One of my favorite villains would be the Joker. I guess I am torn between admiring his crafty intelligence and desiring to see him apprehended. The late Heath Ledger put on a performance for the ages as this prickly criminal dropped puzzle pieces everywhere he went. I have always felt like he was the Riddler's younger brother. He wreaked cerebral havoc on his foes and showed no mercy. Problems, challenges, and trials of life present odds that are difficult to beat. They seem impossible to overcome. They bully us and if not treated, can break us down, destroying us forever. In this text, we see a familiar verse.

David praises Jehovah for how awesomely He crafted him by hand. David was bewildered at the wisdom of God; he was so uniquely put together that it left him speechless and astonished. David was frightened. It filled his heart with awe to see how his personality matured. If you read the previous 13 verses (Ps. 139:1-13), you will see how tangible the LORD GOD's presence truly was in his life. It was out of this divine epiphany that thankfulness, excitement, and love leaped from his heart!

Immaculate: free from spot or stain; spotlessly clean

Has the title of this chapter placed you in a quandry? Does it seem like an oxymoron? If so, I would like to explain. God is far too brilliant to make mistakes. He is completely perfect in all facets and functions. None of us can change our admission into the show called life. I did not ask to be born, and neither did you. I agree with Bob; there are no mistakes. But to take his thought farther, I would add that there are only immaculate accidents. Meaning that what was not planned can be cleansed, what was broken can be healed and operate as if the pain never happened! I believe our existence is not just to exist. We should not spend our years in envy gazing at the "have-it-all-together" family across the street.

We need to look to God and ask Him, "Lord, who am I?" With tenderness, compassion, and love-filled eyes, He looks back at us, pauses, and gently whispers to us while simultaneously sending healing, "You are fearfully and wonderfully handcrafted. You are My divine artwork. Yes, you belong to Me. Trust Me, and I will show you who you are. You are my masterpiece! You, child, are My handiwork. There is no one who has ever been created that is just like you. So, go your way, sin no more, and let Me put the pieces of your life back together again. I will establish you, I will be with you, and I will never release My grip on you. You are unique. You are valuable. You are here for a reason. You are beautifully put together by My hands, and no power or principality, devil or demon, trial or error can wash away what I have written in My book about you. I love you." Through Jesus, accidents come out sparkling! Through His mercy, we are squeaky clean. Humanity past, present, and future has ALL sinned and fallen short of the standard of God (Rom. 3:23).

Even if our parents intended we be born, we still fall short. God wants perfection, and the human family falls short of that. You have read and heard—or even seen in the news—multiple stories of suicide. Young people, old people, famous people, obscure people, rich people, and poor people all conclude that they do not want to be here anymore. Psychologists and other mental health experts have been thrown innumerable puzzle pieces to sort and put back together. Many are stressed beyond measure with attempts to solve the riddle.

Could it be that buried beneath this massive pile of puzzle pieces is a belief that no one cares? Could it also be a lack of knowledge regarding the thoughts

God thinks towards them? Mental health therapists and clinical social workers are necessary. I believe God uses them, but what we need more is the voice of the Lord, Himself. We need to understand that the God of Abraham, Isaac, and Jacob knows who we are! And with His love and support, we can overcome our struggles and have total victory in this battered world.

TWO DARTS

Two of the most devastating weapons our adversary uses against us are discouragement and fear. I don't care if we are saved or lost; he uses these fiery arrows to thwart God's plan for our lives. My wife had a family friend who took his life at only 13 years of age. This adolescent from the inner city of St. Louis had a purpose and a future but was blocked by Satan from seeing it. Witnessing this young man lying in a hospital bed, hooked up to all sorts of life-supporting machines was hard to see. I saw devastation in his mother's eyes. She was utterly brokenhearted. I was asked to visit and pray for him. I wanted and expected him to recover! I prayed the mightiest, most powerful prayer I could. The prayer made the nurses stop walking, but it didn't start up this boy's life again. God had already made up His mind; this time I could not change it.

This boy's death left me discouraged. It threw me into a whirlwind of confusion that took months to get out of. What had he been going through at the time?

Had he been afraid once he'd made the decision to hang himself? Did discouragement bring about this hopelessness? Talking with his mama after the funeral left me more despondent. The parting sight of a teenager who looked as if he were sleeping was way too much for my 27-year-old mind to grasp. It was at that moment I made a lifelong commitment to invest in the lives of young people. To encourage their hopes and dreams. To help them build a bright future. To inspire them to imagine life outside the inner cities of our country, to view the world abroad.

This spiritual conundrum taught me a lesson: there comes a time when prayer will not work. There comes a time when it is all over. We have choices. We should choose wisely! You are too valuable to die. Too gifted to quit! This young man's death could happen to countless families throughout the world, and should serve as a warning and a reminder to discover our value and purpose. Everyone at some point feels sadness over something. We all have a choice to make. Will we be fearful, give in to spirits and voices that lie? What will we do? We must discover God's plan for us. He purchased each of us with His Son's precious, most costly blood. He truly values us in every way! His love for us extends beyond the grave with bright hopes of an eternal future.

It is our great adversary who hurls his fiery arrows in attempt to destroy our faith in God. Ask yourself this question: how many times have I let fear keep me from doing what I should do? Once you answer that question, ask yourself this: when I am sad, how does it affect my ability to move forward? If you have answered these questions truthfully and thoughtfully, you will see instances when fear and sadness stopped your progress. Paul gives us a strategy to counter the enemy. He writes, "Above all, taking the shield of faith, wherewith ye shall be able to quench all the fiery darts of the wicked" (Ephesians 6:16 KJV). Isn't it interesting that the weapons of the devil aim to destroy the confidence given to us by God? Our faith in believing that it has all been settled in heaven diverts every arrow traveling in our direction!

Someone may have said that you are worthless. Another person said that you would never amount to anything. You've tried your entire life to blend in because you wanted acceptance and friendship, only to be met with rejection and enmity. Some of you are the product of an extra-marital affair, others a one-night stand. Some of you were thrown into dumpsters, while others were drug babies. If you are reading this and you can identify with one of these examples, or you are a child of a complete and healthy home yet feel insignificant and flawed, I have good news! God Himself exquisitely handcrafted you! He allowed you to get here, and He is fully capable of making you everything He's said He would.

Block out the inner and outer voices of discouragement, tell fear it has stayed long enough and command it to go! Only when we get sufficiently tired will change take place in our lives. With the help of God strengthening our faith, we can overcome the unfair start to our lives. Do not settle for anything less than what you have felt in your soul is pushing you forward. Never give in to the temptation to quit because you aren't "legitimate." Dreams come true! Don't quit! Whatever you do, don't give up!

DELAYS

Delay: to put off until a later time; defer; postpone
I cringe even typing the word. I will spare you the traditional analogy used after titles and definitions and cut straight to the point. Accidents produce delays in my opinion. When my mother found out she was pregnant with me, her progress and her desires were put on hold. They were delayed. She had to postpone them for me. Setbacks are one of the most challenging obstacles in this life. Our feelings get hurt, our emotions become uncontrollable, we get petty, and on and on. You might have to wait a week for a package you've ordered, but that's no biggie. If it's 10 years, that's a different story. What makes delays worse is when we are waiting for something that should have already arrived.

For years I watched my mom date men who never amounted to anything beyond boyfriends. As a child

I longed to have a father in our home. To me, a father being in my home was a dream. No kid should be forced to equate a father-in-the-home to a castle-in-the-sky. How pathetic. How sad. Yet so many African-American (as well as other ethnicities) homes are left with this sobering reality. My mom struggled to keep all the utilities on. We either had lights or gas or phone. Rarely, if ever, did we ever have all at the same time. You get what I'm saying. Cable TV was a once-a-year perk thanks to the specials they offered at the beginning of the year. We didn't have lots of money. It was hard for my mom raising two boys on one income. God bless my grandparents, aunts, and uncles for stepping in when times were toughest. But deep down, I knew in my heart something should be different.

My dad should have been there. To teach me how to develop patience, how to ride a bike, how to get girls. My dad should have been present. His absence delayed my happiness. So, as you can see, I do not like the word at all. Fast-forward to the present. God, who is perfect in every way, is a fan of delay. I said it; you've thought it too! I don't know if it's the whole "eternity" thing He has going on, but your God does not flinch at those ticks of the clock. In His measureless wisdom, He uses these difficult pockets of time for a reason that only He can explain. I could write an entire book on this subject, but for now I'd like to encourage someone who may be like me–delayed. For good or evil, we are the fruits of our parents' choices. The decisions they have made over the years can leave a mess we clean up. If it took years to get into, it may take years to get out of. I don't like it, and I'm sure you're not fond of it either.

I will get into how I was miraculously saved at 20 years of age later in this book, but when God saved me, I felt everything would change instantly. I was very wrong. It took me years to find solace in knowing my existence was divinely intentional. It took years to become a man. And yes, it took a long time for me to forgive my mother for such a harsh start to life. I spent many years in the "What If Zone." Love should never be deferred. Hope should never be caged. It should be allowed to roam. Some things I feel should not be delayed. Now a grown man with children of my own, I don't hesitate to heap love onto my babies. I celebrate them; I embrace them. I correct them swiftly; I discipline them faithfully. No love can be expressed in a manner that is always 100% pleasing to its recipient.

Love is practical. I find God to be more real world than we want to believe He is. Some things I've been instantly delivered from, while others have been a steady stream of waiting, and waiting some more. Maybe my father's absence cultivated my intense existence in my girls' lives. Maybe the rejection suffered at the hands of family members, friends, and enemies gave me a love that accepts everyone quickly. What we feel is worthless and ready for the junkyard is extremely valuable and handy for the Master. Where Bob saw "happy accidents," God sees "Immaculate Accidents." He can make a purple sky out of a grey one. He can turn clouds into cotton candy. He can take Joseph and give him Ephraim (to be fruitful) and Manasseh (made to forget the suffering) (Gen. 41:51-52). God doesn't need pretty to make beautiful.

He can take any situation, pain of all sorts, problems of every caliber and quantity, break them down, place them on His Potter's wheel, and make something completely new! Let Him immaculate your accidents. Give them over to Him. You don't have to keep them any longer. He is right here waiting for you to surrender them. Time's up for excuses and games. We've wasted enough time. When you get to that point (and I hope it's sooner than later), please throw away your time clock! It's going to all work in His chronology—not yours. At some point in your life, you will be delayed. Yes, you will feel denied at times. I guarantee it.

Please don't lose your confidence in God when it's your turn to be delayed. Trust Him! Allow God to work His work in the order He chooses. If you can bear up under the chafing of time, you will look back and, like the old folks say, "Wonder how you made it over." You will be more mature than ever before and more peaceful than you would dare dream. The devil will be on the run from you! Not the other way around.

From my life to yours, we exist; we are here for a reason. What's done is done, it cannot be undone, but it can be altered by the Potter. Resist the urge to be bitter about your past. Forgive those who have despitefully used you. Loose the person who betrayed you. Not for their sake but for your future. Do it for your health. Do it for your family. Do it for the One who forgave you for so many wrongs committed. The filthy parts of our lives that we didn't plan, the circumstances created by lack of wisdom and understanding, can be recycled if handed to the Omnipotent One! We can't change how we got here. But we can change the direction the mistake intended us to travel. We can actually become friends with hope, joy, and peace and no longer perpetually curious.

THE CHOICE IS ALL YOURS

It might be late, but it's not too late. You are no mistake! You are wonderfully designed with an outcome to be envied! You are precious and worth celebrating. You are someone we need to see. We want to view your talents, outlook, opinions, and personality. We need you! Do not rob the world of your contribution due to something you cannot or could not control. Every one of your life's accomplishments has already been established in heaven. It is waiting to be released in the earth. "For we are God's handiwork, created in Christ Jesus to do good works, which God prepared in advance for us to do" (Eph. 2:10).

It is time to do the good works planned before time by Our Father! It is our time to be used in a greater capacity. Now is our moment to strike the kingdom of darkness with the light of our witness! Our time has arrived to upset the plans hell has for our children. It is our hour to disrupt the strategies of our foes and be victorious in this life! Let us now pressure the principalities and powers! It's time! It's time! It's time!

There are no mistakes—only Immaculate Accidents.

chapter 3

INNER CONFLICT, OUTER CHAOS

"You intended to harm me, but God intended it for good to accomplish what is now being done, the saving of many lives." —Genesis 50:20

F OR ALL INTENTS AND purposes, I should not be alive today. It is by the grace and mercy of the Lord Jesus Christ that I am alive. It is a familiar praise that rises to the lips of many believers, from all parts of the world. My case is literal. As with many of you, I know the devil tried to assassinate me many times.

My mother had a dream of her grandfather shortly before my birth. He was standing closely to her pointing down at me. I was beside him. She took this as a prophetic vision that God was going to use the "accident child" in an immaculate, miraculous way. Her grandfather passed away not too long after this dream, but its effect rippled throughout her early years and has made its way to these pages. When I came out of my mother, I had a thick extra layer of skin around my head. The doctor found it strange but not dangerous. She called it a halo. (Cue Beyoncé.) I came out with something else as well. My hip was out of socket, which forced me to wear leg braces for a short period of my childhood. I got into everything I could as a toddler; you couldn't keep me in one place too long! When I was at the age of a crawling adventurer, somehow, someway, when crawling on the carpet a large piece of metal punctured and embedded itself in my little knee. It required surgery and threatened my walking ability.

Another day, while no one was watching me, I decided to familiarize myself with a boiling pot on my grandmother's stove. The results could have been life threatening. I got up on a chair to investigate the pot–and fell in! I burned my arms badly, second degree badly. Heartbroken, flustered, and upset, my family rushed me to the ER. With wrapped arms and medication, to be comforted by skillful hands, I was sent home. These may seem like incidental injuries that the average kid experiences over time, but I know that they were attacks sent from hell to destroy me!

NIGHTMARES

As a kid I had unusual dreams. Early on we stayed with my grandparents until my mom had enough money to venture out on her own. I loved living with my "Paw-Paw, Gran-maw, and the big tow truck." God blessed them to own a towing company that provided for their needs. They had a comfortable, 4-bedroom home that was complete with a double garage and insulated patio, in a middle-class area in Ferguson, MO. Back in the 80s that was a big deal for a black family. I have so many fond memories of my uncles beating me up (They would say they were making me a man.), fish fries, church outings, and love. My mom's room was in that insulated patio portion of the home. I hated it as a kid for some reason. I dreamt nightmares of green, demonic faces on the walls. They would yell and curse at me and attempt to apprehend me.

My dreams would always go like this: I would get out of bed, and transparent, green monster-like faces would appear on the wall. As I started scampering out of the room to get to my grandparents, these creatures would only let me get so far! Each time I would escape from the patio, race up the steps to the kitchen, and sprint toward the hallway. That's when the floor would become like liquid. It impeded my progress by causing me to sprint in slow motion. Simultaneously I would feel this magnetic pull bringing me back to the patio. It was crazy! Magneto in the room taunting me to come back, or at least it felt that way. These nightmares always felt weightier than a young boy in the land of REM could stand. These dark dreams felt oppressive and prophetic.

I feel God was giving me a warning early on in my life that the events from my birth up until now serve as a hint that the dark side was out to destroy my purpose. The devil tries to destroy us early. It becomes more difficult later. We must pay careful attention to the patience of our adversary Satan; we must be aware of his evil tactics. He loves to prey on the innocent. He makes an example out of the weak. It is always open season for a serial, psychopathic killer of killers to hunt the unprotected. Yet even in my darkest days, I've always felt a light proceeding from me. Looking out for me, providing for me, encouraging me at times. I know it was the prayers of my prayer-warrior grandparents on both sides of my family! I come from a long line of preachers, teachers, pastors, and spiritual leaders.

Leadership is in my bloodline; it comes naturally for me. My mother and father were church kids doing bad things. Church wasn't foreign to either of them. My dad was a Greenlee; Greenlees are a big deal in St. Louis. My granddad has hosted a radio show for years and is the coolest man you'd want to meet. Both of my granddads have swag! But my Greenlee granddad is the extrovert. I never asked him how he felt to have a son have a son so early in life. I imagine he was heartbroken–but loving–throughout the process. Did any of my family ever realize who was created? We can't fault our families for not discerning who we truly are. Things remain mysterious until God sends wisdom and interpretation. What started as a nightmare for both families morphed into a dream for a child.

Growing up it was terribly difficult to shake evil dreams. Another one I want to share occurred when I was around six or seven. In that dream, I was riding in the back of an ambulance. Demons were the paramedics, and they would screech at me to open my eyes. The demons' presence was so evil and wicked that, as a little kid, it was almost too powerful to ward off. Demons hate me. They always have; they always will. Off in the distance, I hear the chastisement of the old-time saints as they awaken to set me straight. I hear them saying, "Baby, they don't hate you. Your name isn't powerful enough to hate. They hate the Name that's in you, the name that surrounds you! Baby, they hate the God who loves you, who blessed you to grow up into a man. It's not about you; God had a plan for your life well before the worlds were formed. He had a plan before plans could plan. So, get it straight. Baby, them ol' dirty, good-for-nothing demons were sent by that ol' dragon, to prevent your destiny!"

I STAND CORRECTED

My point is that, for some reason that I'm still learning to understand, hell has tried to prevent my purpose from maturing. It has challenged my security, my solace, and–unfortunately–my sexual identity. Hear me when I say that I condemn no one in the LGBTQ community. If people believe they were "born that way," I won't hatefully oppose their position. I will say Scripture challenges it; I let the Bible speak when I cannot. When I was 5, a trusted friend on my dad's side of the family sexually molested me. It took place at the grocery store my grandparents owned. All I can remember is being pulled into a small room and kissed and touched. This confused my young-child self and rightfully so. It took me another 15 years before I told anyone. The first person was my grandmother.

This tragedy weakened my masculinity growing up. I wouldn't say I was feminine with a desire for men, but it almost emasculated me as it tortured my developing soul. I lacked confidence growing up in such harsh circumstances, and I became very frustrated with my life. I desperately wanted a way out, but it never materialized. Images and memories of a freaky old man with his prickly bearded face pressed up against my smooth one tormented me for years. I was left with shattered self-esteem.

If you are asking yourself, "Why didn't he tell his mother?" I felt my mom was wrapped up in enough issues. I didn't want her to worry about me. I protected her; I even gave her relationship advice. When she cried, I wanted to make her happy. Moving from place to place, I didn't want what was going on with me to give her any regret. The murkier my mother's life became, the more weight I felt from it. I know I should have told her. However, anyone reading this who has been sexually abused as I was, understands that something about the act immediately condemns us. It makes us believe we were at fault to some degree. We're told, "Keep it a secret," like it's a big game, but it's monstrously destructive in our lives! I'll share more about my habit of keeping secrets from my mom later.

INNER CONFLICT

With a muddled assortment of feelings in my heart, conflict took root in my soul. I didn't know how to share it with anyone. I did what many of us do—I buried it inside. The problem with deeply burying issues within us is that they take up space where love, purpose, and confidence should reign. I don't know if it's an African tradition, but most of our families don't like to talk much about abuse. We just "give it to the Lord." I had no licensed, clinical professional to help me process the pain of poverty and abuse. Some evenings I would sit outside on the front porch and glare at the soon-to-be-set sun. I would cry and ask God to help me. I also wanted to know why I was the one going through so many things at such an early age.

My mother placed a lot of responsibility on me when I was a young child. She worked various jobs that required late nights to be spent away from home. My brother Lynn, who grew up with me in the same house, is five years younger than I am. I made sure he was bathed, fed, and got his homework finished. He was like my little son. Such a crybaby, though!

To this day, he and my mother are as inseparable as they were back then. My brother would lie in bed with my mom for hours watching TV. They shared that bond. For many years I felt my mom did not love me. I don't think it was personal. She just grew to hate my father. He and I are exactly alike in almost every way! It had to be tough raising the son of a guy who broke her heart. Maybe it was too much to take. Don't get me wrong; my mother disciplined both of us, but I felt something extra when it was my turn. When I was a child, she told me that my father didn't want me. Her words broke my heart into 431,000 pieces, and I felt like an outcast. Added to that, it seemed as if my brother could do no wrong.

I still remember being teased for not wanting to work outside with Paw Paw. I hated physical labor. My mind worked like this: I would look at the amount of work needed and assess the time it would take. Then I would calculate how many people we'd have to pay to get it done without our help so I could play. I call thoughts like these "small portals" into what's already been done by God concerning our lives. My family mocked me as a kid. They told me I would have to get a "sit-down job" due to my distaste for yard work. I appreciate their discipline much more nowadays because witnessing my grandfather handle the landscaping on his property has led to me doing the same for my family.

THE DREAMER

I'm pretty sure Joseph felt inner conflict. Born as the favorite son of Jacob, Joseph was treated differently from the rest of his brothers. Joseph was the dreamer of the family. God mapped out his providence and proved it to Joseph by giving him dreams that would come to pass. Parents, be careful to listen to the dreams of your children. Don't discourage their ideas and goals because some of those are given by God! Joseph's dream included his brothers and parents bowing down to him (Gen. 37)! I believe everyone in Joseph's family knew that he heard from God.

If you read this story, you will find that no one ever questioned his connection with God. They took his word as if it came directly from God Himself—and it did! I've heard preachers say Joseph should've been quiet about his dreams; I've heard others say he was foolish for not being discreet with divine information. I'm not going to argue either point because I feel Joseph was destined to suffer before he was crowned governor of Egypt.

Can you imagine telling your family members a secret, having them turn against and report you to the police, and being thrown into jail? To make it worse, Joseph's brothers were far more reprehensible. They not only sought to remove Joseph's presence from the family, they wanted to erase his memory! Be careful when some force comes unannounced looking to wipe out your memory from the earth! Don't take it! Fight back! Joseph fought back with his faith in the words that were given to him when he was 17.

OUTER CHAOS

Joseph is one of my all-time Bible heroes. His story of resilience and perseverance truly resonates with me. He was gifted, he had integrity, he loved his family. Joseph is the textbook example of bad things happening to good people. I encourage you to read his profound story in its entirety because it is inspiring and heart-rending. Betrayed by his own blood, Joseph got a chance to exact revenge for what his brothers put him through, but he offered love and forgiveness instead. Joseph didn't completely let them off the hook. He said to each of them, face-to-face, in their language, that what they had meant for evil, God intended for good. 13 long years of suffering reached a climax for the ages! Joseph removed the dramatics and forgave. Not only did he forgive in word, he forgave by doing good to them that tried to curse him. No chains, rejection, or prison could hold Joseph permanently! His purpose was preordained and fixed by God!

The significance of his story leaves a lasting impression through the years to millions of both believers and nonbelievers. His story has taught me that no matter how awful my childhood was–and let me tell you it was awful–I have no authority to exercise power on my own. Power belongs to God (Psalms 62:11). The outer conflict of my situation is doing good when I want to do evil.

The apostle Paul wrote this: "I find then a law, that, when I would do good, evil is present with me" (Rom. 7:21).

When it comes to dealing with our inner chaos and outer conflict, we have a decision to make. Will we live a life of frustration brought on by our stubbornness and pride, or will we move on from the past while bravely acknowledging its injustices? I'm not telling you that finding good in every situation is easy. It will be one of the hardest decisions you'll ever make; it's probably going to happen more than once. The man who molested me left me with a laceration that leaked until Jesus laid His precious hand on me! Molestation was intended to destroy me as a man. Being run down by evil angels came to cripple my trust in God. Yet looking back, what was meant for evil in my life was used for something good! Something special! So, I encourage you to face your inner conflict when the time presents itself. Snatch peace from chaotic circumstances; identify the positive in every negative situation.

Inner conflict deals with memories, thoughts, voices, and dreams. It has to do with a war within us, tugging us in directions that lead far, far away from God. Handle your problems the way Joseph did. Be loving, patient, and gentle. Resist the temptation to get even; trust that God has already made the way possible to overcome! Parents, talk to your kids, ask questions, look through their stuff if need be. Be careful to never assume that because your child doesn't talk much, he or she doesn't hurt or have secrets. Be involved as much as possible, and above all else, PRAY! Pray until inner conflict becomes internal calm. Pray until outer chaos becomes external harmony. Let today be the first day of your new life!

I'm rooting for you to be the greatest version of yourself possible! I also want you to help others get to that place. What will you say? Will you forgive and move forward? Will you ask God to take the shards of pottery, break them down, and put you back together again? My father told me before he passed away that I was "too big to be little." I echo these same words to you today. Be free from your previous pain; let God make you into something awe-inspiring!

God used Joseph to not only spare his family's lives, but the lives of the Egyptian people. He was responsible for managing two nations, two aspects of the famine (plenty and scarcity), two different points of his life, and finally, two children. What a burden to carry; he had no time for pettiness and condemnation. He was way too busy for that! Joseph was and remains a wonderful example of what leadership is all about. He mixed talent and character with unbroken connection with God to preserve millions of lives. Hallelujah!

I say to you, "Move on from it." Pray and ask God to help you get over the past. Give way to every encounter and opportunity. Reflect but refuel for the journey that is ahead of you. None of us can change how we arrived, but we can alter our departures destined for demise and destruction. Face your giants with courage, and know that God is on your side to remove any obstacles blocking your intended, expected progress! Your deliverance is already sure. Make the decision to resist bitterness.

Inside of you, there is a struggle; outside, there is a war. But it's your time to move on! Will you do it? I know that you will!

chapter 4

OUT MY FEELINGS

"For we have not an high priest which cannot be touched with the feeling of our infirmities; but was in all points tempted like as we are, yet without sin. Let us therefore come boldly unto the throne of grace, that we may obtain mercy, and find grace to help in time of need." —Hebrews 4:15-16 KJV

M Y GRANDMOTHER TAUGHT me about feelings. She would say, "Feelings can fool you." I was a teenager at the time, so it didn't resonate with me. It resounds in me now. Godly grandmothers have that effect on you. They are much wiser than we are, cook better than we can, and have zero chill when it comes to telling us the truth! A common thought among many people is that grandmothers and grand-fathers aren't made "like that" anymore. With a new generation at the helm, we find many grandkids unwatched and loved less due to grandma turning up in the club. Keep in mind that the example of the stereotypical modern-day grandmother is 46, a regular on social media, and difficult to understand.

I'm not sure if I agree with either extreme; I believe reality is somewhere in the middle. I am fortunate to have two grandmothers who both love the Lord and have been granted wisdom by God. They took the time to teach me about God. I learned how to take feedback because of my grandmothers. My grandma Mary would say to me, "Go put some deodorant on! Smelling like a musty billy goat!" She would roast me early and often. Now with children of my own, I appreciate that guiding force of discipline and direction much more because now it's on me to educate and influence my own children. Do you agree with what my grandma said? Have you ever been "fooled" by your feelings? Even if you're not ready to buy into that statement, you must admit that we must not be led by feelings, correct?

FEELINGS DEFINED

Feeling: an emotion or emotional perception or attitude: a feeling of joy; a feeling of sorrow

The part of this definition that jumps out for me would be, "emotional perception." It is safe to say that occasionally, the way we look at things tends to change. We're excited at the car dealership but miserable on payday. Joyous on the wedding day, sorrowful in divorce court. As humans, we are great at starting things; we are motivated and inspired by the launch. But we have much ground to gain when it comes to our habits and work ethic. It's easy to start a diet, but once the smell of cinnamon rolls hits your nose, feelings–they change!

Emotional perception or "emotional understanding" is a very difficult topic to cover. What causes most disagreements and strife? People who "feel" they are right and "feel" others are wrong. We "feel" someone doesn't like us. We "feel" betrayed; we "feel" like we're being taken advantage of. On and on we could go. Our emotions–if we aren't careful–have the ability to cloud our judgment and ruin our logic. The purest part of our makeup is our conscience. It's the seat of integrity within us. It is from that seat that we make or break our lives. So many of us are led away at an accelerated pace to outcomes we never thought possible. We get trapped, and we become isolated. Often bitterness sets in to corrupt our relationships and character.

I'M TALKING ABOUT FEELINGS...

They can get hurt, they can humiliate, and they can confuse us. Feelings are so very apparent in our world today. Everyone gets a platform in today's world to express themselves on seemingly any topic of choice. Some boisterously state their opinions while others are crafty and coy in what they choose to share. Even silence is prompted by a feeling. The feeling of being misunderstood leads many extroverts into using introverted techniques.

Communication is the name of the game. If you are going to be successful in your business and relationships, you must come up with a way to get your message across. Our world doesn't make it easy to convey our thoughts; there's not much room for difference today. Have you noticed how divided we are as a nation? Ever since #45 took office, we've witnessed an array of emotional reactions out there. Just mention his name in the presence of some people, and you will see an immediate emotional response. Mention former President Barack Obama to some circles, and the same thing happens.

From pundits, to athletes and celebrities, right back around to the church, politics, and corporate America, emotional reactions are predictable. I have no desire to be led away by what I feel is occurring. If someone betrays my trust, I've learned that it is best to immediately make the choice to forgive. Once I make that decision, it is final. What isn't as straightforward is how I feel towards that person.

I believe this is an area where the devil is successful in attacking us with condemnation. He accuses us of being unforgiving towards our neighbors; he justifies that accusation using our feelings. But I believe that we can totally, completely forgive people yet still feel some lingering resentment. Over time that feeling changes, but the forgiveness was there the entire time. How exciting is that? That I don't have to trust my senses to believe what is true is a revolutionary concept. The joy is overwhelming to know I have confidence beyond anything I was ever born with. None of us can change what's happened, but if you are a born-again believer, you have the power to not be led astray by what you feel.

JESUS WAS TOUCHED

In our next text we look at another familiar passage that deals with the role and office of Israel's high priest. A high priest in the Old Testament was the highest human religious leader of his people. Aaron (Moses' brother) held this high honor with his sons expected to follow in his footsteps. The high priest was distinct from his fellow priests by the clothes he wore, the duties he performed, and the hallowed responsibilities placed on his shoulders. Although the office of high priest was ancestral, the possessor of this tremendous office was to be blemish-free and holy in all aspects of his character (Lev. 21:6).

He wasn't allowed to show grief for the dead. He was never to remove his headdress, and his hair had to stay well maintained. If his mama died, no grief was allowed. If his dad died, same rule. His garments could not be ripped, even in personal loss.

If there was a dead body in the area, the priest was not allowed to go near it. However, the high priest was not prohibited from marriage, as long as it was a "virgin of his own people" (Lev. 21:12). His marriage had to be above reproach as well. If the union were not, it would contaminate the lineage. Priests had zero room for error. One glitch carried fatal consequences just as it did for Aaron's sons (Lev. 10:1-2). As we can see, the priest weren't really "touched" by the feelings of the people–or even their own. They sacrificed for atonement, or put another way, to make God less angry with His children, but that is as far as the connection went with the masses. I can just picture people attempting to hold small talk with the priest on their way up to the sanctuary. Sort of like the Queen of England's guard, they were not having it!

Simply put, God's people had no one to relate to them. Ever been there? We feel misunderstood in various ways, on multiple levels, at times in our lives. Our pain has an expiration date we know nothing about. Until we are released from it, our pain usually gets worse before it gets better. Without an advocate to speak up for us, we are left to fend for ourselves, isolated and broken. This ministerial barrier ordained by God placed His children in a state of dependency upon appointed officials to present their missed marks before God for judgment and compassion. Just as God forgave the sins of the nation of Israel, our pain has a time frame in which it must leave!

I used to wear my pain around like it was a Cubanlink chain. I just knew nobody understood what I was going through. When you grew up in a dysfunctional environment, Aaron knocking on your door seems like a fairytale, let alone the Almighty being concerned. I grew up in church and noticed as a young boy how God moves upon His people, so I knew He was real. But when it came to individual, personal life, that was a different story for me. My mom was the leader in our home. At that point in her life, she didn't lead us in the way of the Lord. It left me with a need, one I couldn't provide for in my own power or time frame. I needed a real-life hero who understood where I was, who I was, and what I was thirsty for! I was in search of Jesus.

JESUS KNOWS

Unlike the high priests of the Old Testament, Jesus not only knows all points of our pain and brokenness, but He became pain and brokenness for us (2 Cor. 5:21). Here's a savior who is a Super Specialist when it comes to handling pain and our sin. He was born in the likeness of humanity, yet he was perfect. Jesus came to His own people. They weren't waiting for Him with open arms (John 1:11). Born in the humblest circumstances, King Jesus arrived with one purpose in mind: to save humanity. There were no thunderous trumpet blasts or the procession of a mighty army at the arrival of the Holy One. Jesus bypassed all the pomp and circumstance of royalty to sit with His creation. No tabernacle, for He alone is the sanctuary. His flesh the veil hiding the glory of God. It was He who took on the form of a servant, to serve servants who wouldn't serve the Server! I encourage everyone to read how fundamentally unpretentious Jesus was when He lived on earth. It is the understanding of our Lord's humility that leads us to receive from Him.

STARS?

Have you ever met a celebrity? Celebrities are people we celebrate for their extraordinary feats, accomplishments, and talents (or number of followers). Every celebrity needs a fan to validate his or her status. No one can be celebrated without an audience. At least this is true in secular society. Without dropping any names, I've had the privilege and–at times–inconvenience of running into famous people. The ones I hold dear would be those who were relatable and unassuming. I felt the opposite emotion for the arrogant idols. I would say to myself, "Who do they think they are? I buy their such and such, watch their such and such!" What drives us crazy in these moments, I believe, is that human beings who are afflicted with some of the same weaknesses we are treat us less than we are worth.

These are the ones we deem "stars." The multimillionaires and even billionaires, the 1%. I've never been envious or intimidated by rich and famous figures, and I find myself praying for them often. It is hard to see what a person is going through when you don't live in their sphere. Jesus didn't take this approach when He came to us. He left the furs and all the shiny jewelry back home. He even left His security in heaven! Oh, I know you remember the soldiers He put on notice (Matt. 26:53). Emmanuel, the once-in-forever and indestructible phenomenon, left glory, and dwelt among us.

The greatest example that we'll ever know did the unthinkable, loved us on our level. With this most important knowledge, we can walk up to Him with great confidence! He already knows our human frailties yet desires to have fellowship with us! If we are overly timid, come boldly; if we are overly confident, still come. Let nothing prevent you from approaching God to obtain all that you need. If you're a celebrated figure, at some point you will need to come. I don't care what everyone else thinks and says of you, you must come! Let not the opinions of men keep you from being touched by God. God feels your hurt, and He understands why you can't trust anyone. He feels your isolation and shame.

People don't lose their dignity when they come. There is plenty of room for all. Come just as you are: no facades, no masks, no concerts. Just come. Earthly shimmer fades over time; our kids are destined to replace us. We can only hold on to the glory for so long in this world. Life pushes us out of the way at some point. I sympathize with athletes who mentally still have it yet are physically ill-equipped. Obscurity comes at some point in our lives, and we never welcome it when it arrives. That's why it's critical to develop a legacy with God. Leave our mark in our time that inspires in every direction. Our kids need to see our boldness; they should sense our passion. They may not understand it, but they should recognize our pursuits.

You may say, "What is boldness?" I'm glad you asked! If we are to boldly come to the throne of grace, if our outcomes are already worked out in heaven, boldness is key to maintaining sound emotions during difficult stretches. Grace is the key to remaining outside of our feelings. We must take a deeper look at this word "boldness."

BOLDNESS DEFINED

Boldness: all outspokenness, frankness, bluntness, assurance and confidence

Wow! I get excited just reading a few of these words. If we are to obtain anything from God, we must truly go "all out." I cannot recall how many times I've heard people complain that God isn't real. Or, if He truly exists, why would He allow all the world's issues? That's a thought packed with pressure, hurt feelings, and emotion. Behind most of these statements–in my opinion– stand people who haven't learned to press their way into God. It could be attributed to a lack of experience or frail confidence.

If we are to ever move past this atheistic thought and dive deep into the abyss of grace, we must go all out.

Like all the way out. The first step is removing ourselves from complacency and identifying when it is
time to make a move. Once we agree to move, we must
be consistent. This life is about doing things before
they happen. We must portray confidence before it en-
ters our hearts. We must speak differently and think
differently! We must separate ourselves from negative
influences that discourage us from coming to God. We
must believe it's done before it is done!

20 YEARS OLD

Oh! When I was 20 years old, God's love compelled me
to come to grace. He patiently pursued my broken heart
and boldly declared it was healed. He recruited me as
if I were His #1 pick. He passionately laid out a future
for me that was beyond my most ambitious imagina-
tion. He trusted me with revelations that couldn't be
uttered! I had to come to Him, and He wanted me to be
blunt about it.

I got tired of living the same old life; I wanted to make
a change. I wanted out of my feelings. I wanted out of
my surroundings. I wanted out of my isolation. I wanted to break free from inner demonic powers that bound
my soul. I got tired and determined enough that I was
willing to do whatever it took! If I had to stop smoking weed, I would do it! If I had to stop chasing wom-
en, so be it. I was a prisoner to my emotions, and if the
God of the universe was beckoning me to come to Him

because it's already done, I was in! I didn't waste any time either. Some of my family members were used by Satan to say it was just a scare into religion. Others said it wouldn't last. 21 years later, it's still here!

The moment we make the move is the moment we experience liberation. We don't have a high priest with a high mind who cares nothing for us. We don't have a priest who's preoccupied with temple duties. We have a priest who feels us! Hallelujah!

CONFIDENCE

I get compliments on how confident a person I am now. It wasn't always like this. I was dangerously insecure as a child. I hated the way I looked and was teased in every level of schooling. I was first-picked for nothing and abandoned often. With that kind of background, it's easy to see why my mindset was such. I was a victim of bullying; my uncles taught me how to defend myself physically, but I never learned how to brush off verbal insults. Once hurled in my direction, they would shatter my security. I wanted to be accepted and liked as we all do from time to time. Something deep within me would whisper to me that things would one day change for the better. I had the silly idea of closing my eyes and saying to myself as a 'tween, "On the count of three, when I open my eyes again, I will be brand new!" That's a cute and ambitious idea for a youngster, yet I had no power to sustain it.

Have you ever been there? Wanting change so badly yet when pressed by darkness revert to what is familiar. I witnessed behavior front row in my mother's early life. In the times we did visit church, she would get so convicted by the message that once we left the service, she'd throw her cigarettes down the sewer! But just a few days later, we're back to reality. What a state of frustration! To know we need to change but have no ability to produce a lasting outcome. What disillusionment to come boldly to our sin yet timid to our deliverance.

The moment I was filled with the Holy Ghost with speaking in tongues my life changed eternally. Please don't mistake me; I still had to learn how to refrain from sin, but something drastically transformed my innermost being. Instead of timid, I was bold! Afraid to speak up no more. Now I challenged everything! I hurt people's feelings early on unnecessarily, and for that I apologize, but a warrior erupted in me! I went from sinful to set-apart. Puny to powerful. Wretched to righteous. Bitter to sweet. In one single, solitary moment I was suddenly alive and unafraid to tell anyone who would listen. My deliverance, though miraculous, was simple. Jesus wanted me, and I came to Him boldly! I didn't let what my family or friends said deter me; I didn't let my flesh or the devil control me. If there was a way out (and there was), I was taking it with no looking back! I had to leave what I perceived as comforts and pleasures at the time. Now many years later I view them as aggravations and trouble. This is what grace does to a soul. Not only does it redirect the person, it redefines!

With old things passed away and all things made new (2 Cor. 5:17), I took that scripture literally and ran for my destiny. I'm not into living a second-class life. I want to live in all the fullness of what the Master prepares for me. He's already established every word I will speak, counted the number of steps I will take on this earth, and disarmed every power that thirsts to control me. I believe with all that is in me that God has a future prepared for me, and I let nothing or no one thwart my progress. My advice to you would be this: trust God, walk up to Him, and tell Him what you need! If He went through all that grief and sorrow to have fellowship with a flawed people, what more needs to occur for trust to rise within you? Get up! Get out! Get what you need! Take it! Move towards it with confidence! It's already yours, and it's already done!!!

When I meet new people, they think I've always been confident, but what they misunderstand is I am a product of the grace and mercy of our Lord and Savior Jesus Christ. I am an instrument in the hands of the King to be used for His good pleasure. I never shy away from my testimony. God has increased my confidence because I boldly approached Him. I took what I needed for my soul! His delight is to see us whole, healed, and free. It gives me a great deal of confidence to know someone is always truly cheering for me. Someone has my best interests at heart in all matters.

God has felt every pain, pressure, burden, and insecurity I have ever experienced. God understood the depths of my pain, bitterness, and loneliness. He didn't observe my suffering from heaven's gates, shake His head, and give orders to His angels to tend to me. No! What Jesus did for me was far more commendable! He lived His life as the Son, carried my burdens, and took my sins away! I deserved to be punished, but in the end I prospered. He reached way down into the swamp I called home, pulled me out, cleaned me up, and told me He loved me. He didn't hold my past against me. He didn't rebuke and condemn me. God wasn't punitive towards me, and He should have been.

Don't you know that He may tarry, but if God has marked you, it's only a matter of when, not if? It was His precious and most costly blood that scrubbed away every foul and polluting thought! It is His blood that prohibits me today from living by what I feel. His blood makes me come home to my family each day instead of chasing impressionable women. His blood has kept me out of scandals, and His blood works miracles in my life today.

My grandmother was right; feelings can fool us. They limit our development and impair our vision. We must take our feelings—the good ones, the bad ones, and the ones we aren't sure how to label–to the One who felt complete abandonment on our behalf. We must put away our shyness and break free from seducing spirits.

There came a time in my mother's life that she put away the cigarettes for good. Our deliverance from sin isn't just for ourselves! On the contrary, our deliverance gives hope to all who surround us. When the Lord radically changes our lifestyle, it inspires. That's what happened to my mom in 1998. Addicted to crack cocaine, struggling, and in her feelings, I told her about what Jesus did for me. I explained how aggressive I was to get to Jesus. I told her it was my time for healing, and I wasn't bashful about it! Even though she gave birth to me, I opened my mouth and declared the gospel to my heavy-hearted mother. God granted me the pleasure of witnessing her being filled with the Holy Ghost! Hallelujah! The mom and son who bought drugs together at one point in life now are free from the power, presence, and penalty of sin. Two souls who came boldly to the throne of grace. Taking what we both so desperately needed.

It's your turn to get up from where you are and go! You must because living outside of your feelings once and for all is a heavenly appointed possibility. Jesus has already suffered for you to be free! Your deliverance is here, my friend. Don't wait any longer. It's already done! Get yours!

chapter 5

MENACE TO SOCIETY

"Foolishness is bound in the heart of a child; but the rod of correction shall drive it far from him." —Proverbs 22:15 KJV

IT WAS ONE OF THE MOST thought-provoking movies I had ever seen in my young teenage life. *Menace to Society* was an instant classic in the 90s. It starred Jada Pinkett, Tyrin Turner, Larenz Tate, and a host of other talented actors that we know and love. This movie depicted gang life in the streets of Los Angeles, particularly the inner-city projects. Caine was an ambitious 18-year-old with dreams of making it out of the hood and steering clear of becoming a statistic. Caine's best friend O-Dog was the opposite of Caine. O-Dog was America's worst nightmare. Young. Black. Heedless. Without any regard for the future.

We would call him a savage in today's America. O-Dog was a natural-born killer. Many could argue that he was a product of his environment. Caine's committed, thick-skinned, witty girlfriend, played by Jada Pinkett, wanted the best for Caine, but the streets kept calling his name.

Caine would eventually learn the hard way that it's easier said than done as it pertains to planning and execution. Escaping for him ended up only being a wish and not a reality. This movie placed an impression early on for me that in some ways I still feel today. You see, I wanted to be a gangster growing up. The lifestyle simply fascinated me as a youngster. It was this sort of black male that gained my attention and respect early on as they ran the streets and lived by their own set of rules. To me they were broken yet untouchable, flawed yet flashy. They happily played the role of villain in an American society that portrayed white men as the only heroes. True to form, through the wages of sin, I developed a bad habit of stealing.

When my mother was chased to Minnesota in the mid 80s by her fire-breathing, crazy ex-husband, my habit only grew worse. Living with rebellious, demon-possessed, in-law cousins fueled my thievery. My eldest cousin-in-law would make me, a 9-year-old, run into gas stations to do snatch and grabs. I had a fear complex towards anyone I deemed stronger than I, and it almost cost my younger brother and me our lives. (I'll get to that story a little later.)

Each time I would walk into these stores, I'd look around and notice the clerks busily tending customers with beverages and requests for gas. With the smell of freshly cooked hot dogs in the air and this new music genre called "hip hop" blasting from the radio, I went to snatch and grab Garbage Pail Kid cards.

I won some battles and lost many. Often, I ended up in the back of a police car with merciful cops who took me back to my disgusted mother in the inner-city Minneapolis projects. One time she told the police to keep me because I wouldn't stop stealing. I never told her the backstory: the threat of being beaten if I didn't come back with the cards.

One time my oldest cousin sent my cousin and me to steal some acrylic paint. We were unsuccessful, and he made us pay dearly for it. This demon-filled teenager, who was gifted with drawing, made us stand in a closet for hours, punching each other in the face. I'm talking closed-fisted haymakers thrown in close range. These blows couldn't be blocked; if we did, it would only get worse. This monster, or I should say, "menace," enjoyed watching us beat the life out of each other. With tears in our eyes from the pain, my cousin would take his turn beating me, and I took mine beating him. At one point I remember my cheeks being so swollen that I couldn't close my mouth! My mother held a night job at a nearby Days Inn, so supervision was next-to-none. I hid my wounds and pain. Each time that I had bumps and bruises I'd lie and say we were playing outside.

HOUSE OF HORRORS

I 100% hated living in that house. I was exposed to pornography, lost my virginity to my girl cousin-in-law, and almost lost my young life. The menace choked me violently–too many times to count–in his great rage. The abuse got so bad that I started pretending I was dead, so he would drop my body to the ground, and I could catch my breath. This horrific time period left me perplexed. I couldn't understand what I did to deserve it. He got so good at abusing that he gave these times a name: torture time. He would tell me I was going to get tortured. I was thrown in a washing machine and dryer (turned on) and placed inside of a suitcase that was thrown down steps. (Laugh if you must. It's okay.) He would spit in my cereal and demand I eat it. If you're screaming, "Why didn't you tell anyone?" I was deathly afraid. Plus, I wanted to protect my mother.

I remembered the bruises on her face from being slapped by her husband. Her shrieks of horror resounded loudly in my 6-year-old ears! I saw her get punched so hard that she stumbled into the next room seeking shelter. She escaped from St. Louis to her in-laws in Minnesota. I felt if I told her about the horrific circumstances that surrounded me, we would be left without a place to stay. So, I naively endured the suffering, and it almost proved to be fatal.

ANGELS ARE REAL; I CAN PROVE IT

At the age of 8, I was alcohol poisoned by my extremely abusive cousin. I remember eating corn, mashed potatoes, and chicken for dinner that night. My cousin mixed a concoction of dark and light liquor, plus he threw in drink mixers as well.

"Drink it!" he barked.

"No!" I screamed back.

"Drink it, or I'm going to hurt you!"

Fear won this round, so I drank it. After drinking every drop, I became heavily intoxicated.

He panicked and told my other two cousins, "Take him downstairs to their room."

My mom, little brother, and I lived in the basement of this project townhouse. My little brother was asleep, and Mom was working the night shift. After I was thrown onto my bunched blankets on the cold cement floor, I started to get sick. I began to throw up violently as any kid exposed to liquor for the first time would. I was so off-balance that I had trouble rolling onto my side. Lying on my back, the vomit began to fill my lungs. As I lay there, choking, my 8-year-old spirit was pulled away from my body. It was an intense and bizarre feeling to hang between two realms.

My praying grandmothers had no idea the dysfunction their grandbaby was facing. My destiny was on the line. My life was in jeopardy. God sent an angel to help get me out of the mess I was in! With my hope put to the test, I needed mercy to snatch me out of this situation. I didn't see wings or halos. The room didn't become blindingly light. I just caught a glimpse of glowing feet and the bottom of a robe. Then the most tender of hands–like those handling a newborn baby–rolled me onto my side. When this occurred, my spirit snapped back into my body! I coughed uncontrollably; I was hurt and injured–but alive! I developed a profound respect and admiration for angels that day. Nothing can shake my confidence in their existence.

Don't get me started about this "already doneness" of God!

He sent out His word concerning me before the world began. There was no way I could have died on that cold, Minneapolis floor. When you receive a word from the Lord and believe it, nothing can stop you! I didn't see it that way then; I just wanted to escape this snare against my soul. My mom was oblivious that I was persecuted. The devil caught a glimpse of Whose I was and fought me on every side! Before I could spell the word "attack," it was upon me. Thank God for your angels, and thank Him for the price He paid for you on Calvary.

DARK NIGHTS AND EVEN DARKER DAYS

I share these experiences to prove God's great love toward us in any situation. I am aware that these are extreme circumstances, but I want someone to be free. I want you to know that no matter how dark it gets in your life, there is hope for you today because of what has already been accomplished for you! Never forget the boundless power of Calvary that transcends generations and time, all orchestrated and implemented by God–for you and me!

My days would only grow darker after this miraculous deliverance, as we lived in this adverse corner of the globe. Satan possessed my older cousin; I felt nothing but evil when I was around him. In one of his days of rage, he beat me with a baseball bat because I didn't steal some paint from school. I was so afraid. My other two cousins were ordered to hold my arms as he viciously swung. I can't recall how many times I was hit, but it was too many. I lost the strength to stand, collapsed in the middle of another swing of the bat, and suffered a blow to the face. One of my teeth went through my lip. My cousins panicked as blood gushed everywhere.

"What do we do?" asked one of my younger cousins.

"Grab some shaving cream!" ordered my oldest cousin.

Yes, they tried covering up the gaping hole in my face with shaving cream. Alarmed, my cousins rushed me up to my bed and laid me down—as if rest would heal me.

"Tell your mama you fell down the steps when you were sweeping!" yelled my oldest cousin.

My mother came home from work shortly after this incident, and as you can imagine, she was horrified at what she saw.

"What happened to you?" she yelled.

Dazed, hurting, and losing more and more blood by the minute, I said, "I fell down the steps when I was sweeping."

"You did what?"

"I was sweeping and fell down the steps, and my tooth went through my lip."

"How is that even possible?" yelled my mother with tears in her eyes and despair in her voice.

Later, I said, "I did fall, Mama, that's what happened. I'm so sorry I put you through all this trouble of taking me to the hospital."

I was rushed in for emergency surgery, and after 100+ stitches, my wobbly face was put back together. I remember overhearing the conversation that the surgeon and my mom had about my recovery and future. My mother was afraid I would never look the same again. She was so discouraged. I would've been too if that was to happen to one of my kids.

"Will his face get better?" my mother cautiously asked.

"Yes," said the doctor, "But it will take years for his lip to regain normal form. He will be an adult before it does."

As I lay on the gurney, all I could think about was my mother. I never blamed her for not being there to protect me. My mom was everything to me, and I wanted her life to be painless. This predator, whom I should have reported, was free to wreak havoc in our family. If you're a young, abused kid, speak up! Don't be like me. Tell somebody before you get killed. Don't allow predators to roam our streets. Speak up and speak out. God will help you!

I still have a scar on the right side of my face as a reminder of my past. God–yet again–yanked my life from the strangling hands of those awful relatives! I love Him so much for what He did that day for me. I no longer carry the pain of my childhood. I've reached a place in my life that forbids me to think back for too long. To share these stories is difficult for me, but I have been redeemed by the power of God! Sin no longer reigns over me; the past is done!

You would like to think that after this mind-blowing, life-threatening event that a sort of solace and normalcy would set in. The fact I didn't rat out my cousins should earn me some respect, right? Wrong! It's one thing for the devil to attack you personally, but when it's a beloved family member and you must watch it, it is truly heartrending. At another time, I was forced to sit down and observe my little 5-year-old brother get choked by my demonic older cousin-in-law. I felt so powerless as I sat unable to aid him. Like I said before, he was like my son; I had protected him up until this moment. When his eyes rolled back into his head, my cousin threw him on the bed and ordered me to help him. My brother went into a forced seizure from the loss of air. At this moment, my mind went back to a CPR class that I had taken at school recently.

An instructor had come to our class and taught us the Heimlich maneuver and a couple other life-saving techniques. I was born with the ability to catch on to things quickly, so I put it to use. I wiped the foam from his lips and began to administer CPR. It felt like days, but I'm sure just a few precious minutes went by. My brother's pupils and irises came down out of the top of his head, and he regained consciousness.

I take no credit for this; all I know is God used me to do what I could not accomplish on my own. My grandparents' prayers were put to the test, but they prevailed! Thinking back, I'm not sure why my brother was picked on that day. I was the object of their hatred 99% of the time. I am so thankful that God intervened and allowed my brother to continue his life. He suffered no ill effects from the attack, and life went back to "normal."

THE BREAK UP

When you are a little child, you pick up on dramatics, but as far as why they're happening and the details, that's a different story. My mother became part of a lover's quarrel with the family we lived with. She became romantically involved with her in-law's man. This drama reached its height forcing us to move from downtown Minneapolis. I was ecstatic to leave this den of death! I was done with "torture time" and "meanness on, meanness off." Meanness on and off was a game where I could be mean to my monster cousin and was then told to stop. Sick right? Terrible times for my young soul. I was relieved to hear we were moving out of the hood! People talk about how "hood" they are, but unless you've lived in projects where there is blood on the elevator floor, illicit sex, gang affiliation, and drug use, you don't know what you're talking about.

My mom ended up landing a good job in Eagan, Minnesota, so we decided to move there. Packing up and preparing to leave gave me the smallest impression of what liberty felt like. My cousin was very upset, and decided to leave me with a "going away present." He placed a fork on the flames of the stove until it was glowing neon orange. He rolled up the left sleeve of my t-shirt, and branded my shoulder like I was cattle! As my flesh burned, he said to me, "This is so you'll never forget me." I screamed, but he didn't care. Two years of extreme abuse were ending. I'd endured much pain–handfuls of salt thrown into my eyes–and trouble–making me punch a hole in my mom's waterbed because they hated her–in that dark townhouse.

Maybe the times of sitting late into the night, gazing at the stars and the moon, and mournfully asking myself what I did to deserve such punishment would be over. I believe the devil tried to destroy my voice during that time. He knew I was a future communicator, so he tried everything God would allow to eliminate my mission and my dreams. It is my belief that darkness attempted to assassinate this future leader.

FOOLISH SILENCE

My error in all these stories was my willingness to take it on the chin for what I perceived was the greater good. In no way should I have ever kept silent. I call it a "foolish silence" because if not for God and His abounding mercy, my life would have ended before my 10th birthday. Who knows what my mother may have done in those years? I'll never know. I never gave her the opportunity to protect me. My silence screamed louder than the blows that wailed upon my small frame. The scripture that leads off this chapter deals with error found deeply within the mind of children. The Bible says the rod of correction drives foolish behavior far from them. A rod is firm, it is consistent, it can be depended on for delivering mood-changing behaviors. Used rightly, a rod can give us life-changing results. I'm not saying God used a rod against me, but I am saying my own inability to report my abuse to someone left me in need of correction. I learned from this time how effective words and communication are.

Parents keep watch over your babies. They are born with foolishness in their little hearts; it's no fault of their own. Handle your business and protect your little angels, so that they don't end up with a childhood like my own. Discipline your future leaders. Give them hope; encourage their curious minds. Let them dream the impossible, but most importantly, be very careful who you allow to keep your kids! I don't care if it's close family members; guard your children at all costs. You may lose hours on your paycheck. Lose them. You may be around them longer than the average parent. Be there. It may get on your nerves that you can't get anyone to keep them from time to time. Be upset. Take the suffering so that your children can run free.

Don't wait until it's too late, or you will regret it for the rest of your life.

PRAYER FOR PARENTS

God, I lift every parent that reads this book up to You. Lord, give them wisdom in the handling and raising of their children. Let the weak parent be strong. Let the poor parent find true riches. Bless the single moms, so they find balance. Let them also have rest and peace. I give you praise for raising up parents that will be rods in their children's lives, driving the foolishness far away. Jesus, bless fathers to not grow weary in being the leaders of their homes. Give them courage and well-paying jobs to lessen the possibility of their kids getting into trouble by lack of parental supervision.

Bless every parent in Jesus' name.

Amen.

chapter 6

QUIET DISRUPTIONS

"Speak not in the ears of a fool: for he will despise the wisdom of thy words." —Proverbs 23:9 KJV

B Y NATURE, I AM A TALKER. It is sure that I was put on the earth to communicate. I'm also passionate. I am emotional. I express myself best through my words. I want people to know where I am coming from. My intention when I speak is to leave no doubt as to what I'm attempting to say. My mouth has helped people; my mouth has hurt people. I've shared some heavily weighted moments in my life with you that hardened me as a person. In some ways I'm desensitized; in others I'm exposed. Yet what lies in the middle of this continuum is a deep desire to be understood.

Misunderstandings are inevitable, because at some point we will say something that gets received far differently than what was initially intended. I told you about my inability to speak up for myself early on. This was a huge problem for me that almost cost me my existence. However, when I came to Jesus, I discovered my voice; I found my purpose. Once I found my voice, there was no going back! I knew I wanted to be used by God to spread His message of love and eternal life to the world. This was a big dream for a small kid from St. Louis.

It's amazing how God takes what's considered the least in life and uses it greatly. Words are incredibly powerful. There were some words spoken to me as a child and some as an adult that I will never forget. My pastor back home, Bishop Johnson, used to say, "Be careful what you say because you can put drops of dye into the water, but you can't take them out."

Our society readily forfeits the power of its words by its unwillingness to act on them. Promises are words with expectations attached to them. I have a strong dislike for unfulfilled promises. To me it is far better to never make the oath to begin with than to make it and break it. Hope is often deferred due to the absence of actions behind words.

When a person gives me their word, it's like covenant to me, though far from the agreement God makes with man. A person's word is directly associated with their heart. If we are liars by nature, it will show up through what we say. Daily we face two choices: to be foolish or wise with what we say.

Our lead-off scripture deals with the words we choose to speak to those who place minimal value on them. At first glance, you would think it encouraged total separation from fools. There's a deeper meaning to this prudent piece of advice from above.

I believe it deals with identifying the foolish one first, then once we recognize them, falling back from revealing information. This is a difficult task because to be honest, we don't always make wise decisions. We let the wrong person leave with the right information, only to throw what's dear to us in the trash.

MEASURE TWICE, CUT ONCE

Have you ever heard of the expression "measure twice, cut once?" It is one of my favorite sayings. It means that if you are going to make the decision to separate jointed materials, think twice before you cut. I am attempting to get you to notice how powerful words are yet how weak they become once they are used in the presence of people who despise wisdom.

The easiest way I can define wisdom would be "making smart choices in every situation, all the time, due to divine insight." A thought pops up in our minds to do a certain thing or say something timely. We use the smarts given by God to lead godly lives. New sense in our heads breaks forth! I am learning as I get older how to quickly distinguish between wise and foolish individuals and be smart when I open my mouth. We get one time to leave a favorable impression, make it count! Many of you have visions and dreams. Deep within your heart lies a tug or pull. What you are feeling is purpose keeping you from becoming settled in a place only meant to be a stop.

Once I was filled with the Holy Ghost, I was filled with zeal and purpose! It ignited in me an endless pursuit to become what God gave me a small glimpse of. I told anyone who would listen to me about my dreams. I was so eager to get to a destination that I had to be reminded by those who despised my hopes that life's a marathon. I was unwise in sharing; I needed to learn how to keep it private. I didn't know then what I know now: God whispers the impossible in our ears for His good pleasure. Outcomes rarely turn out like we envision countlessly in our minds. Many plans are in our heart, but it's God's purpose that shall stand (Prov. 19:21).

QUIETLY

God is into silence. When I say silence, I'm not referring to the absence of sound. It is my belief God wants to do amazing wonders in our lives that remain secret until the appointed time. God works on our behalf–if we allow Him–through quiet disruptions. You and I have an enemy who pursues us and attempts to swindle, lie, and cheat us out of our purpose. He throws fiery darts of confusion and doubt that fly at break-neck speed. Just as soon as we block one, another one comes.

The barrage of weaponry hastily hurled is intended to stop our progress. We cannot let that happen! We are in a war. A war for our faith. A war for our families. A war for our destinies. If you ever get to a place where you see these as something worth fighting for, keep that mentality until the day you are called to glory!

Your God and my God loves to disrupt things. A disruption is an event, activity, or process that causes a disturbance or problem. It means to break up an order. For this disruption to take place in our lives, we must settle our spirits and listen to what He will tell us. We take our enemies by surprise when we settle down, and listen to God's instructions for lasting success. Even the ones close to us may intend good for us, but they do not have omniscience. Their aid won't disrupt; their presence temporarily comforts. If we get serious enough, if we get angry enough, we can see some things change in our lives! Don't waste your time giving the details of your dreams to those who don't have your best interest at heart. We lose time, effort, resources, and energy when we open our hearts to the wrong people.

Fools want nothing of value in life. They live for the here and now; fools partner with our enemies to destroy our purpose. Fools waste their years on fleeting pleasures that create eternal bondage. One more thing

I will share about fools that you may not know is that they don't always appear to be fools. Many of them sit in high places. Crowds may adore them and hang on their words, but any person who abstains from the wisdom of God makes a foolish choice.

There will come times in your life when God orders your mouth to stay closed on a situation. It's the exact opposite of the "Open your mouth and praise Him!" we hear each Sunday. As much as it hurts, don't get injured by sharing your dreams and visions with the wrong audiences. Pray about it and check with God for what He will say next to you.

It's all about timing with God. He strategically plans to use your life to disrupt the powers of darkness in this world! Yield to His leadership, pour out your heart to Him, and let Him lead the way. God's disruptions won't be quiet after He's finished, I can assure you of that. When He decides to act on your behalf, He will confuse your enemies. He will strip them of the power to harm you, and what they meant for evil will be used for good (Gen. 50:20)!

We by nature are creatures of communication. It is in our DNA to share information, especially with those we love. Words expressed are hearts articulated; it is common order. God, in His divine wisdom and sovereignty, made it so. Due to the fall of our parents, Adam and Eve, the lines of communication became tangled. We've been attempting to untangle them ever since.

It amazes me that no matter how many times we cry out against injustice, come up with solutions to fix bad neighborhoods, and strategize ways to revitalize undeveloped areas, the notions are rejected by those who appear to be wise. Disorder and chaos are more suitable than organization and tranquility. We are broken.

Please remember that it's not the words alone that garner the angst of the despiser; it is the wisdom found within them. You have heard the expression, "Don't kill the messenger." Well, it's the same here. The underlying problem with our words comes from the wisdom that is stuffed within them. To make what I'm saying clearer, let's say we share with someone advice or insight that can give hope to their lives, but they must first separate from that man or woman who causes pain. Smart people will agree with us because of the intelligence in what we say. Yet those who are foolish quickly get upset, throw down your advice, and curse you out!

I believe this scripture deals with this sort of example. We must choose to refrain and leave room for God to do His work. Remember that it's already done! God has already gone before us and set the stage for our successes, triumphs, and losses. We have the victory over the darkness of uncertainty! Keep looking towards heaven to encourage your journey and path. If your friends don't see it, forgive them; if family fails to recognize your purpose, love them. Leave your words before the throne, and watch God perform wonders. Pray for clarity and insight as to whom to reveal and whom to conceal your destiny. I can promise you that if you throw off rejection, you will soar on wings of eagles!

Just because we face rejection does not mean we are rejected! Learn whom to trust with your dreams and visions. Everyone can't handle who you are. All can't understand your testimony. When the world sleeps on you, God is there giving you the grace to push forward despite living in the company of fools. Do not get discouraged when people despise your sound advice. Please do not let what they say dictate what you will do. The decision is yours to make today. Believe God that your destiny and purpose are already done. The more you believe it, the more you become it. Choose to believe!

chapter 7

SILENCE IN THE COURTROOM

"And at midnight Paul and Silas prayed, and sang praises unto God: and the prisoners heard them. And suddenly there was a great earthquake, so that the foundations of the prison were shaken: and immediately all the doors were opened, and everyone's bands were loosed." —Acts 16:25-26 KJV

IN THE FALL OF 1994, I was a sophomore in high school. With no father in the home, the title of provider went to my mother who unsuccessfully attempted to fulfill that role. Our ends never met: utilities were always a luxury, and the streets were calling my name. I joined the neighborhood gang called the "Six Deuce Crips." I felt acceptance, and it took my mind off the conditions I faced in school. We chased women, fought rivals, and some of my gang mates sold drugs. It was a moral struggle for me to walk down any of these paths because I knew better. I did have a love for the ladies, but I was too nice to fight (too little also) and too afraid to sell drugs. In my neighborhood if you got caught with even the smallest crumb of the blazingly popular drug crack, it carried a mandatory 5-year prison sentence. No questions asked!

I had no intention of spending my life in prison. America would not bat an eye if I chose that path, but it wasn't a life I wanted to live. I remember listening to 2 Pac, Biggie, NWA, Spice 1, E40, etc. I wanted these artists' glory, but not their stories. Thug life for me was baggy jeans, do rags, house parties, women, drinking, and drugs. Half of the neighborhood would hide on the side of my house until my mother left for work. We waited until she left to party! My friends were bad influences on me. I didn't hang with people who knew God. I had no maturity at that point in my life for "words of wisdom." I was a young, semi-wild man who was blinded to his purpose and destiny. If the words "It's already done," were whispered at my spirit in that stage of life, I would have blown them off.

SAINT LOUIS THE DIVIDED

When you think of "St. Louis," what comes to mind? Is it the peanuts and Crackerjack that you find at our Cardinals games? Or maybe it's Nelly. Is it Cedric the Entertainer, John Goodman, or maybe Sterling K.

Brown? These hometown heroes as well as our beloved baseball team leave an impression in our minds that is true, yet incomplete. St. Louis–for some– is extremely enjoyable, entertaining, and wholesome. Others feel it's a place of racial chaos, bitterness, division, and disorder. To many, it's the land where your kid can get shot and authorities get off for doing it. For some it's a city that is progressively working itself back to the days of Jim Crow and segregation.

I lived in St. Louis for 30+ years of my life. There are lots of cool people from various ethnic backgrounds who reside there. I have many friends who live in STL. It is a melting pot of education and community, but we are a segregated society. One of the major confirmations of my statement rests at the Delmar Loop. On one side you have the affluent; on the other you have adverse poverty. They are separated by a stoplight. With redlining, racial profiling, and discrimination, I found STL to be a possible place for black men to make it, yet a frustrating one for many of us.

God will bless any human being that loves Him in any location of our world! But growing up in this city made me feel like the world matched our animosity. Our school systems were segregated, and I'm talking about the early to mid 90s. From Rodney King's unjust treatment to the OJ Simpson trial, the divide in my city has always been evident. From news reporters spewing out racial epithets with just enough undertone to avoid job loss, to unfair taxes in various parts of the city, St. Louis is prosperous for some and challenging for others.

It was there in my hometown that my destiny was forever changed as a young teenager. There was a battle that tried–yet again–to destroy my future. This time it presented a different challenge. Unlike my previous brushes with death, this death was for my social security. It would ultimately change my life and those of my family forever.

SCHOOL DAZE

I attended public school in the Ferguson-Florissant school district for middle and high school. Coming back to St. Louis when I was 12 was a culture shock from Eagan, Minnesota. I got teased a lot in school for speaking like a "white boy." I hated school! Buried underneath the bullying, peer pressure, drugs, and social groups lies the expectations of gaining an education. Coming back to live with my grandparents was different as well. My grandparents were the loving bridge to me getting to know Jesus.

Good comes out of every situation if we let it. I struggled with my grades in certain classes. History was a stretch because I always felt that the story was told from one viewpoint. I was interested–yet not impressed–with half-truths. I excelled in music, art, and mathematics. These subjects came naturally for me. I still use each one of them often. I'll get into my talents in later chapters.

I was a young man full of hormones, hurt, and hang-ups. Amid the meanness of my peers and the racism from some teachers who felt too good to teach black children was a determination to acquire learning. I pray so much for youth that are in extreme poverty situations in one of the most affluent countries in the world! Young black children are undervalued in our society. We are left with shrewd legislation set against our advancement that leaves us bitter and broken. When it comes down to it, some of us view education as the "white man's thing," because we have been long denied full access to it. Before my wife and I made the decision to leave St. Louis, we pulled our children out of the community's failing school system. We felt we could do a better job, so we became homeschooling parents for 4 years.

It was this system that made the decision easy for us. I wanted better for my girls. They did not deserve to be treated as I was. It was in the mid 90s that I found myself an impressionable, curious teenager. Even though I was sort of chubby in middle school with dry hair and a bad fade, I was my daddy's child! Deep down inside of me was his swagger and style. The conditions I faced back then made it very difficult for these qualities to come out. Never judge a book by its cover; you may be pushing away your blessing!

In high school I faced full-fledged racism. There was a time in my sophomore year that I ended up in a very racist science class. My friendly, outgoing personality was met with a hatred I never saw coming. It was in this science class one day that I attempted to joke around with one of the white female students. Her contempt and hostility towards black people was unknown to me.

I was outnumbered in this class full of entitled students with a bully mentality. Being my joking self, I tried to say something harmless, but she was not having it. This girl pushed me and said, "Get the **** away from me. I hate n*****s." I was shocked! This had never happened to me with such blatancy before. For some reason I have always held a cool head in moments of adversity. I believe it's a God-given temperament that keeps me calm. I didn't push her back or curse her out. I walked back to my seat after it all calmed down. She also told me to "Go back to Africa." And, she ended her hate with a popular phrase.

The teacher did nothing, the students never spoke up, and I never reported it. Each one of us was wrong in some manner that day. Though I was the victim, it would have been better–looking back–to fight it through the help of the principal and counselors. I was so embarrassed by this situation. I could not understand why people would hate me without knowing who I was. I've never felt shame for being who I was. I embrace who I am and have grown to do more of that the older I have become. Hatred is too big of a hurdle for me to jump. I choose to love.

MIGHT AT MIDNIGHT

Our scripture deals with the Apostle Paul and his protégé Silas. On the way to prayer one day, they came across a woman who was demon possessed. This woman was given powers to predict future events. She took this ability and created a lucrative business for herself and local partners. Paul commanded the spirit to leave her body, and it did! As you can imagine this deliverance proved bad for business causing the local authorities to throw Paul and Silas in jail for doing what was right.

The will of God leads us at times to difficult places. Don't let anyone fool you. We cannot minister to people who hurt if we ourselves have never experienced discomfort. I would not say that God orchestrated the imprisonment of His faithful servants, but He did allow it. I love what these men of God did in jail. I wonder if they ever had a clue we would use this unjust experience–and its miraculous deliverance–thousands of years later!

If you will notice in scripture, Paul and Silas weren't just patted down, talked to roughly, and then thrown into a cold cell. No! The Bible says they were severely beaten, even flogged! To be flogged is to be struck repeatedly with a whip If I were there, the last thing I would have strength to do is sing. I would pray; I would also intercede for my enemies. But sing? Sometimes to get what we need from God requires a praise unlike any before. Sometimes it takes a different approach to opposition. Their singing was more than a peaceful protest; it was a cry to the God who said all our victories are already accomplished! It was a distress signal! The best thing that we could ever do in our dilemmas would be sounding the alarm for help.

"Help us! Help us!" Maybe their singing began with a cry for help but ended with the glorious name of Jesus being lifted! Paul and Silas sang about God's bigness! They refused to allow chains to separate them from the love of God. The way I envision their miraculous outcome is they began faintly their song of praise. After a quiver, strength began to form in those bloodied, chapped, parched lips. A noise was released that reached the throne of God. Their disturbance touched the heart of God, and He commanded angels to see to His boys. Their deliverance was already set in order before time. There was no way they could remain chained!

I'm not sure if it was a melody in unison or a two-part harmony. All I know is it was fervent and effective (James 5:16)! The Bible said at midnight there was a quake that shook the jail, it opened doors, and it set the men of God free! Each of us should pray such a prayer that our worship would rattle the foundations of our problems, open doors of opportunity, and set us free from what binds us. I have personally witnessed this magnitude of prayer in my own life, but I wasn't the pioneer of it.

THE SCHOOL SPLIT

In one of my sophomore classes I was attracted to one of the white girls who sat next to me. It was just lust to be honest with you, nothing emotional about it. One day as we sat next to each other during the playing of a video, we began to touch each other. This mutual touching was mixed with notes being passed back and forth. Little did I know that every note I wrote was saved to be sent to the principal's office. Something consensual ended up being the exact opposite. We only touched, never kissed, never had sex. This wasn't a big deal to me. Like I said before, I was a 15-year-old with hormones. I'm not saying that all teenagers think the way I did back then, but some do.

One day I was pulled out of class to head to the principal's office. He proceeded to tell me that this girl reported that she was sexually abused. I said to myself, "Sexually abused?" I was deeply afraid because growing up I heard all the stories about what some whites in power do to young black males. I was devastated that someone who touched me just as I did her would do this to me. It was unbelievable.

I lied to the principal to try to get out of trouble. Too late. It was upon me. I was walled in. Completely blindsided and humiliated, my situation went from bad to worse as they called in the police to question me. It felt very 1960s. I was interviewed for hours with my Momma at my side, getting her heart broken just a little more each time the clock struck a new hour.

These police didn't care for my kind. As a minor, I was publicly handcuffed and walked out in front of half of my schoolmates who were having lunch. The officers and school officials used me as an example of what would happen if we ever "crossed over." Our school counselor, who was also African American, was horrified at the mistreatment. This was such a low point in my life that it made me question my future.

It was also during this time that we were struggling financially. My mother's drug habit contributed to the poverty. It was the middle of winter, and we had no lights, gas, or phone. My counselor, so touched by my story, visited our home. She was overcome with emotion as she witnessed our breaths coming from our mouths as we spoke. It was so cold in our home that she looked up at me from our living room couch with despair-filled eyes, and pleaded, "Baby, put a coat on."

I've heard people say that they didn't realize they were poor growing up. I can relate because it wasn't until that moment, I figured out what a mess we were in financially. I hated it but endured it because my mama always said she had a plan. I felt for her having to provide for two young men. I did what I could through working to contribute, but I cannot say she spent the money on bills entirely.

During this adverse time, another controversy arose. I was with a young girl who got pregnant but ended up losing the baby, so she says. Being young and in love can make you say things that aren't true if you're not careful. I took it as the truth and added it to the mounting pile of issues I was too green to handle at 15.

The family of the young lady from school sought to not only charge me for the "crime," they wanted me charged with 2nd degree sexual abuse. Outrage broke out among the staff of my high school. Many teachers couldn't have cared less what was true or false. I felt they had been content to watch another poor, young black male leave "their school." They even got a bonus watching me get handcuffed and escorted out of the building during the busiest time of the day. I was guilty until proven innocent with all the intensity a man twice my age would face.

I was officially charged with 2nd degree sexual abuse for touching a woman who consensually touched me. To make matters worse, the prosecutor requested I be registered a sex offender for the rest of my life. My family was crushed. Out of fear, I continued to tell them that I never touched her; it was so blown out of proportion that it left me overwhelmed. I couldn't believe this little church-going boy, who overcame so many obstacles growing up, would have to stand before a judge who would possibly see him, an offender and the girl, a victim.

WON'T HE DO IT?

This was a very perplexing time in my life to say the least. I wasn't exactly "close" to God at this point but I did pray. With the gang banging, women chasing, and drug and alcohol lifestyle, I felt unworthy to approach the throne to ask for mercy. After the investigation was completed, after the charges were filed, I was formally expelled from my high school with detention school as my only option. This event hit me like a single-engine plane crashing; I was wounded and bleeding. My mother ended up losing her Section 8 housing subsidy, which forced us to find a small apartment nearby to live in.

With scheduled court appearances cancelled each time they were made, this process went on for six months. I found it odd at the time that I wasn't going before a judge. It was an abnormal pattern; something was at work. I was shackled by accusations in a dungeon of discrimination and racial prejudice, and I could not find my way out. There was no human solution for me. I was trapped and needed an out!

Eventually, my mom ended up losing even the apartment we lived in, so I moved with my uncle. My Uncle Tonio was tough but loving and provided a stable life for me. I respect my uncle for taking me in and teaching me how to be a man. This began a shift in my life that was bittersweet. My court situation was still up in the air, my girl said I got her pregnant, I said goodbye to my mother and brother, and I was jobless. But God!

One day as I began settling in with my new family, I wrote them a letter expressing how much I appreciated them letting me stay with them. I was happy–yet sad–because my family was still out there struggling. As the months progressed, I found out my girl-at-the-time allegedly lost the baby in a volleyball game. I was hurt to hear the news. It added insult to injury. Locked away in a cell of uncertainty and desperation, I called out to God to deliver me from the problems I was facing. My grand-mothers throughout this ordeal would periodically talk on the phone and intercede for my freedom. I didn't know it at the time, but I'm glad they did!

Out of nowhere, one day I received a letter in the mail saying that the case was dropped! It gave no reason as to why; all we know is that the family had a change of heart and decided to drop all charges! I was a free man! No scandal, no future as a registered sex offender. I was free indeed! I remember kissing every floor in my un-cle's home and celebrating. (It wasn't a holy celebra-tion; I wasn't there yet.)

This miraculous deliverance taught me about two things: the power of prayer and the supremacy of mer-cy. Even while I was in my trespasses and sin, God was still concerned about me. I feel He loved me then as much as He loves me now!

Let my story inspire you to begin again. Even if you were wrongly accused and it went the distance, trust God to put your life back together. Give Him all the glory for the victories! Had it not been for the Lord–who was on my side as a teenager–I wouldn't be here today sharing my story with you. I am grateful to God for producing silence in the courtroom of my affliction! He never let me stand before a judge and eventually let me walk away free.

I can't say the experience left me without scars. It did. I didn't hate white people before, during, or after it, yet it spoke loudly in my ears that racism was alive and well. I began to guard myself more. I dated only within my culture. I vowed from that day my wife would share the same culture as I did.

Our experiences have so much to do with the shaping of our personalities. This time in my life sobered me; I feel like I lost a lot of my innocence. It taught me to be very careful and trust God until the very end! If God did this for me, He will do it for you also! Cry out to Him in your misery and brokenness. He will step in and push you forward. The reason the prosecutors fully failed to prosecute me was because God destined that I would be a leader! He determined before life lived to create me for His good pleasure and purpose. It was already done! No devil can stop us when we know what has already been set in stone for us by God's amazing love. Check the paperwork! Our outcomes are fixed!

God commanded the legal system and the family that wanted me so badly, "Silence! There will be no harm added to My child's life." He set me free. He will deliver you! Your jail will quake! Your chains will break! You will go free!

chapter 8

BEFORE MY DEBUT

"For the vision is yet for an appointed time, but at the end it shall speak, and not lie: though it tarry, wait for it; because it will surely come, it will not tarry." —Habakkuk 2:3 KJV

(FRESH PRINCE BEAT DROPS.) Now this chapter is all about how my God picked me to rock the crowd. I'd like to say it happened before I lost my hair, but I had to wait for years, and those years felt unfair!

"Wait! Y'all getting on my last nerve!" says the mama in the kitchen fixing Saturday morning breakfast for her impatient children.

"But, Mamaaaaa, you said it was almost ready," whine the petulant, emotional preteens.

"You don't want no half-cooked bacon, do you?" challenges the mother.

"But we're hungry, Mama!" insist the kids.

The battle ensues, yet there will only be one winner–Mama! Even though she is frustrated, the kids done got on her very last, reserved nerve, she understands that relinquishing her plan risks sending her kids to the hospital with a food-borne illness. So, during this emotional whirlwind, the mother keeps her stride and runs her household. If a natural mom with no connection to God gets what to do for her children, how much more the eternal God who knows everything?

A TIME-MEASURED LOVE

We connect God's love to time. I've done it; you've done it. Any person who is just that, a finite being in the universe that resides on planet earth, has felt the weight of time. We are bound by it because we are subject to it. Eternity isn't based on the past, and it's certainly not about the future. Eternity is always occurring, it's never going to end. It has no origin, but it originates. It isn't futuristic yet foretells the future. It is perpetual, perfect, permanent fellowship with God.

It is God; it emanates from His being, aggressively pursuing any soul that lacks it. Don't feel bad for the lack of insight on this one; eternity is something else! Our minds are too puny to grasp the heftiness of such a topic. We are children of brevity. Our end starts at the beginning. We are born to die. The more we age, the more definite that outcome is no matter how healthy and wealthy some of us find ourselves. Our bodies were born with an expiration date, yet our spirits and souls last forever!

We are subject to chronological order instituted by God Himself. We cannot alter time because it is transient. It steps into each of our lives like an opportunity and escapes like a thief in the night. Time is precious to all; we can never get enough of it. Have you ever lost a loved one? Don't you wish that you had more time with him or her? Do you ever think about that person coming back into this world if only for a moment to speak with you? Maybe just a smile and a gentle touch would do.

We can accumulate all the assets life has to offer, yet time is irreplaceable. At the time of this book's writing, my youngest daughter is age 6. She's still little enough to be picked up in the air yet innocent enough to believe her dad is a super hero. As I glance at her world, I realize that the nature of our relationship is changing day by day; I grieve what was. Time sometimes intensifies grief. It has the potential and capacity to affect our emotions. Thanks, Adam. Thanks, Eve. It's no fairytale or myth. Through this couple's disobedience our lives are forever impacted by time.

Without time there can be no memories; without time there can be no predictions. The older we become the more evident it becomes that we must make the most of our time! We have a charge by God to be fruitful in our seasons (Ps. 1:3). It is important that we think deeply about what we spend time on and how to maximize each moment.

LIVE EACH DAY LIKE IT'S YOUR FIRST!

I'm pretty sure you have heard the phrase, "Live each day like it's your last," or the equally popular, "YOLO!" (You only live once.) What a frightening way to live! I get the sentiment, but I still think we should look deeper. To me those statements promote reckless, wasteful, gluttonous living. A mentality of this nature breeds irresponsibility and develops frivolous attitudes. If I were to live each day like it was my last, in the eyes of the world, I would be bold. I would appreciate each day as if no more were coming.

What if we adopted the opposite mindset to achieve greatness? My logic says that if we must wait, let's make it pleasant. What if we lived like each day was a brand-new start? Each new day came freshly wrapped, and each of these days eagerly anticipated our unwrapping it! I know some of you reading this book are saying to yourselves, "Dre, I don't get it." My idea isn't as far off as you may think! Hardships make us hesitate to look at life from the viewpoint that each day is a gift and should be anticipated.

Habakkuk was an Old Testament prophet whose patience for the wicked Chaldeans had run out. Under King Nebuchadnezzar, Babylon was the absolute wickedest city of its day. Powerful and prominent,

Nebuchadnezzar's reign upset Habakkuk to the point that he questioned God's sovereignty. He wondered why God would use this wicked nation to chastise His children. This prophet grew weary. While the Chaldeans became more affluent and oppressive, Israel suffered.

Our text in this chapter is a promise made by God that the demise of this kingdom would come at the appointed time. We hear the heart of the prophet crying out for God to sweep the land with judgment (Habakkuk 1). Our country needs God to sweep the land with justice. With racially disproportionate numbers of inmates, homeowners, leadership positions, and crime statistics, we are a nation who needs God again! We cry out unanimously in tragedy yet fragmented in triumph.

I cringe at people who proclaim themselves prophets yet lack justice in their hearts. It is saddening to hear of someone who holds this office yet refuses to see the hurt in our world. This should not be. God promised Habakkuk that He would work a work in His day that he would not believe, even if it were told to him (Habakkuk 1:5). The promise was real, but it seemed so far away.

IT'S TIME...KIND OF

Growing up, I had a love for music. Amid the violence and cruel and unusual punishment I experienced as a child, God gave me a musical ability. I am a lyricist.

I love word play and rap music. Back in the day when we had tapes, I would wait until the end of songs, and record them on a blank tape to create an instrumental track. I was good at making beats. People in the hood loved to hear me play on toy pianos and beat on desks at school and my front door at night in our little cypher battles. I was good at free styling; it came natural to me. We would battle for fun, but the lyrics that came out were raw, pure, and real. God let me know at a very young age that music would play a huge role in my life as an adult. I didn't have the resources to nurture my gift as a kid, but it felt good to share, and I wanted more of it.

The first time I rapped in front of a large crowd, I was 14 years old and at a local skating rink. They invited anyone who had hot bars to come out on the rink and spit! The only rule was to not use profanity. My friends hyped me up to get out there. I walked out in front of the crowd, the instrumental running through my body like a cool breeze on a summer evening. Nervous, sweaty, drunk, and a bit high I began spitting my hot 16. All I remember next is getting booed off the rink and escorted expeditiously toward the door for–you guessed it–using profanity. Even though I took an L that night, my confidence soared in a way it never had prior. This was a sign of things to come.

Not everyone noticed or encouraged my love for music and creativity. I had some skills, but I was not the most talented individual growing up. I took either a music or band class each of my years in school. Some of my classmates gave me props, while others said I couldn't rap. When it came to women, if I liked a girl, I would often express my interest through writing. Some girls accepted it and others didn't, but I had a love for making others feel better and admired through my words.

When we accept God's call in our lives, we must walk within our callings humbly. Many of us who were chosen by God were rejects by the world's standards. Most of us did not come from a background of limelight and exposure. God expects each of us to trust Him to use our talents for His glory and to approach Him for direction. So many times, it's the exact opposite of that. We turn what is meant for the betterment of the church and society inward, creating a downward spiritual spiral in our lives. I know for myself God would allow me to garner a little shine then it would fade away. It was a "Now you see me, now you don't," season. It was difficult to wait for the vision to come to pass when I didn't understand God's entire process.

In 2003, I was introduced to Christian rap, and I was underwhelmed. I grew up listening to the greats, so listening to people who were trying to figure it out confused me. The beats and lyrics of these artists–I won't name any names–were flat and outdated. A friend of mine, who's gone on to be with the Lord, hipped me to beat making. He gave me some artists to listen to.

One day in the hottest part of the summer, I sat in my car angry at the lack of passion and talent on these CDs.

It went something like, "Why can't people rap hard for the Lord?"

As I sat there the Spirit spoke to me and said, "Because I want you to do it."

"Me?" I screamed.

"Yes, you," whispered Jesus in the most loving way imaginable.

"Oh, no, not me! If You want me to do it, I need to sound like no one who's done it before! I can't be whack, God!"

"Okay," said God.

From that moment in that vehicle with the Almighty, I began to take music making more seriously. My friend mentored me in beat making, thus my gift as a rapper took shape. Yep, 16 years ago I was called by God to do music, and I have yet to see consistency in that area of my life. Who can relate? Has anyone ever had a promise given but not yet delivered? Were you excited because the God of Abraham, Isaac, and Jacob picked you to be the one?

That's usually the first reaction to a promise given by God–excitement and joy, but what usually follows is bitterness and disappointment because of the waiting process. Habakkuk felt the weight of oppression in his day and the glory for his people. He knew God was mighty and performed signs and wonders, but none were evident at this time of his life. Convinced his generation was subject to doom, he questioned the integrity of God.

It is easy serving when life doesn't force you to ask questions. This wasn't the prophet's case. He was frustrated. What I love about God is He doesn't leave us in our discouragement. He sends us comfort and hope! God let Habakkuk know that greater days were ahead even if they had to be waited on. I love how upfront God was with the prophet and me. He never promised me overnight success He never promised accolades and awards. He simply asked me to go, and I did.

What I want you to take away from this chapter is this: purpose is already done. We just need to get in agreement with what God has for each of us. When He asked me to do music, He asked me to get in line with what He had already predestined for me to become. I'm so glad I said, "Yes!" You will be glad too, and many of you already are! Though completion of the vision delays, please don't give up. It may take 10-25 years, but learn to appreciate your development. Serve the Lord with gladness. Admire the progress you are making, even if many days you feel the opposite. Fight for your faith! Hold on to it. Never let it go! It is your ticket to your future.

God presented small beginnings to me, and to be honest, I wasn't very fond of them. I wanted to be used in a greater way. I wanted my way, and I wanted it right away. I'm telling you it has not turned out that way for me. Every time it seemed like I was gaining ground on the vision, it felt as if the delay was extended. I was hurt by what I saw as a lack of headway. I began to connect God's love to timing–my time. I put Him on a timer, and He just looked at me and smiled when the clock hit zero. My "right now" was His "not yet."

If many of you are truly on the path that God laid out for you, it will challenge your theology. You will see what the Word says and begin to grieve because your life doesn't match up. You will also question whether you heard from God altogether! John the Baptist declared Jesus the Lamb of God, which takes away the sins of the world. Yet when pressed by opposition, he was tempted to retract his proclamation (Luke 7:19). Real relationships are intense and full of emotions. They honestly get the best of us at times. We all must improve on that area of our lives.

In my wait, God wanted me to know that before my debut there were some things I needed to learn. There were doors that needed closing in my life as well as discoveries I had to make. He wanted me to know that family is greater than fame. He wanted me to understand that man changes, but He remains the same. Before we run out to save the world, we need to identify what may be a threat to our souls. We must master our discernment of what sorts of lusts draw us away from a godly life and lead to a broken existence.

Waiting is a discipline of the soul. But thanks be to God I did not give up on the process! I'm so thankful for honest leaders who shared how their own waiting felt unfair. I'm grateful they spoke to God telling Him that they felt it was unfair, and wondering why He was treating them this way. I've heard so many "It's your time" messages throughout the years that I became seemingly numb to them. I sighed at the smallest amount of encouragement that would come my way because in my eyes, nothing but seeing the promise fulfilled would satisfy me. Boy, did I have a lot to learn.

Though what you're believing for is delayed, wait for it! You are not waiting for something that needs to be created. You are waiting for what has already been created for you way back in eternity past. Know without any doubt whatsoever that God's plans and purposes for your life will surely come to pass at the right time! Before you make your debut, get acquainted with the One who has already seen it. You will be so glad you did!

chapter 9

HE KNOWS MY NAME

"Before I formed you in the womb I knew you, before you were born I set you apart; I appointed you as a prophet to the nations." —Jeremiah 1:5

A S I BEGAN TO DISCOVER more and more of my God-given abilities, I didn't know how to use them. God blessed me with a talent that was taboo in church at the time. I joined a group called "G-Crew." That's short for "God's Crew." No gangsters here, only very sweet people who went out in the community spreading the message of Jesus through music.

Gerald was our leader. I'm thankful for his no-nonsense approach. He taught me how to master the unexpected. When we would rehearse, G would pull out our mics on purpose. He would stop the tracks, anything to throw us off our game. I hated it! He was a person that I allowed to coach me. We can refuse the assistance of many leaders in our lives, but with G it was different. It was here, along with my local church, that God began to sharpen my stage presence.

At the beginning I wasn't terrible, but I wasn't developed either. I've always been brave–but cautious. The funny thing about growing up the underdog is there is no pressure. You aren't even on people's radar. To them you are a "nobody." After seeing so many pulpit personalities it was hard finding my place. I knew God had called me to preach, but He was taking me on the scenic route. I excelled in seminary, but during one year He told me to quit. I was confused why He was asking me to throw away so much time and effort.

Llechor and I had very little money, a '98 Neon that was on its last leg, and a toddler! I scrimped and saved just to get into the school, and now God was pulling me away from it. Or so I thought. I have always been a Bible student. I'm sure you've felt a little of that from this book. It's just who I am. I love the Word of God because it is God Himself. Music became much more of a priority to God than education at this point of my life. But, I was confused because not many churchgoers supported it.

I worked like crazy to perfect my craft. I studied endlessly trying to maximize my gift. I remember the first time I messed up my words on stage. I was crushed. No one else knew it, but I did, and I was so hard on myself. I got up from the fall, dusted myself off and kept going. Far from record deals and lucrative offers was a young man pursuing a dream and a passion. When you pursue what you love to do, money becomes secondary. I performed at lots of events for free. It took years before I was ever handed any money. I didn't care. I had tapped into something deeper than eyes could see, and I wanted more of it.

THE UNDERPUPPY

There are underdogs, and there are what I call "underpuppies." An underpuppy is a person who not only faces insurmountable odds but isn't supposed to be near the battle at all! I, for some strange reason, have never fit into any group. Much has never been expected of me. I'm not revealing low self-esteem. Nor is this a lame attempt to seek sympathy through a false sense of humility. I am describing my life the way it was and has been. The reality of it all is that, until very recently, I didn't comprehend why I was put on earth. I felt like my mother and father's lives would have benefited from me never having entered the world.

My sister and brothers, except for my second-oldest brother who–like me–was born out of wedlock, came from purpose. I felt cursed. I felt that what could go wrong would go wrong. As a black man in a predominantly white-run society, I was needing a reputation. We as humans love to label things. We get it from our father Adam who had dominion over the earth and named animals within it (Gen. 2:19-20).

We judge people by what they produce or fail to produce. We pounce on the ones who have "issues." We sometimes bury them deep within our own frailties and insecurities to make us feel better about ourselves. Is that the root of prejudice and racial discrimination? It's debatable. But what is not up for debate is the fact that puppies are weak and incapable of self-sufficiency. Puppies cannot nourish themselves. Has anyone treated you this way? Has your gift been minimized? Is there anyone reading this book who's been the object of criticism and judgment? Let me encourage you to push past the lies and accusations, to really press in to what's already been prepared by God for you!

SUCCESS THAT BRINGS CONFUSION

God has not forgotten about us! I still fight obstacles and haters. At the time of this book, God has placed me in a position that I naturally do not qualify for. There were far more qualified candidates, yet the opportunity was exclusively for me. The world has never seen anyone like me! The world has never seen anyone like you! The reason I got the job is the same reason you got yours. We got our success because it was already decided before we got to it! Don't you know that God wants to use those who are not considered wise, strong, or eloquent (1 Cor. 1:26-30)? God purposefully allowed my life to take the shape it has so that He can be glorified. God will bless our lives in such a great measure that they will literally throw everyone around us into confusion.

The underpuppy became the roaring lion! The last became first. The tail became the head, and the least became great. Hollywood makes billions off scenarios like this, but this is far from a fairy tale. It is a reality. I want to live in a constant state of favor and blessing. I want my misery to be turned into a ministry. Don't let any devil near or far push you into a corner of mediocrity and pain. Get out of your comfort zone to see what may be right there in front of you. Tell the devil goodbye and run to the One who knows you!

BEFORE

Our passage deals with the young prophet Jeremiah who was handpicked by God–before he was born–to be a prophet unto the nations. He accepted his call with great terror. His book is about the certain judgment of God upon Israel for rebellion and disobedience. Because of idolatry and sinfulness, God's wrath was predicted to strike the Hebrew nation in the form of slavery. Jeremiah continually strived to turn the people back to God, but they never did. Jeremiah feared not being respected because of his age (Jer. 1:6). The

Lord corrected him for thinking this way and reassured him that he was the man for the job. God used one word to throw Jeremiah off psychologically forever. That word was "before."

Before: in front of; ahead of; in advance of

Basically, God told Jeremiah this: "Jeremiah, who you are came before where you are. Who you are was known well in advance and ahead of time. Jeremiah, your calling and personality were created ahead of your body. Jeremiah, before you could choose a vocation, My will set you apart from your family, friends, and peers." What words to share with a teenager! We sometimes get it confused that church is about older people, but here we see something different. Here we see purpose projected onto the prophet which empowers him to accomplish great things.

As a 20-year-old young man with a desire to serve the Lord, Jeremiah was one of the first books I read. His life gave me so much confidence that God knew who I was and wanted me to know it. Even though Jeremiah didn't receive the happy ending to his life we all would want to give him, I'm pretty sure as he stepped out of exile and into eternity, he did so emphatically praising God! Whenever you get to a place in your walk with God where you find it a privilege to suffer for Him, you know you've tapped into something! I've always felt impressed to believe that if I read the Word, I must practice it in my life. I must strive to live it out if I am to see God's blessings in my life. The book of Jeremiah was just that for my life. God knew Jeremiah's name.

BEFORE IS BEFORE!

It takes faith to believe that "before" fits our lives. Many challenges, setbacks, and obstacles attempt to make us forget about it. We cannot afford to throw away our "before." It's critical to claiming every victory we will ever have! When we don't believe people are telling us the truth, we shut down in some way or another. Their words and voices become smaller and smaller in our lives. Day-to-day we test their character until something proven or logical happens. If we doubt God's "before" in our lives, we doubt the endless depth of His intelligence. Be very careful and pray often to remember there was a "before." "Before" kept me from going to jail. "Before" protected me from having kids out of wedlock. "Before" took me home at night. It helps keep my mouth closed at times. It helps me fight devils with great confidence that I've already won every contest! It will make us ask questions. It will make us search the scriptures. "Before" will set us off in a direction that leads to answers from God Himself! Aren't you thankful for your "before?"

ENDING HAPPY

Life does not promise us happy endings. Death snatches many people away faster than any of us care to see. Life has multiple degrees and variances that make it difficult to navigate. Having the assurance that God knows who we are will keep us before His throne. He knows everything about us and still loves us! What love! God knowing my name really says He values my reputation. God not only searched for people who are responsive, He looks for those who are willing to keep a good reputation–for life! 100% can't be done alone.

With His help, our end will be satisfying. I believe Jeremiah left this world a happy person. Excited, he finished his race, moving on to a world of comfort and joy without end. Jeremiah accepted the great challenge put before Him, while being reminded that God went ahead of him. His outcome resulted just the way God intended. Purposefully wonderful!

Imagine living in an era where the glory of God was missing, and the people were doomed to judgment. God often calls people to proclaim a message that other people will never listen to. Incredibly heartbreaking and painful to imagine. I hate correcting my children over and over, so I can't imagine an entire nation's rebellion.

Just because my beginning started in turmoil, my ending does not have to match it. I will finish strong with my latter being greater than my former (Hag. 2:9). I find so much peace in this journey called life because I understand that God knows my name. He knows me! The God of the universe knows exactly what He's doing in my life including the setbacks and disappointments, problems

I can't fix, bills I can't pay, and visions I can't fund. God knows. I'm glad that Jesus is a wonder in my soul!

Make sure that you don't miss out on your "before." It is this knowledge that prompts current peace and holds us until we see future blessings. What a joy to know that we don't have to worry about our futures and have lingering shame over our pasts! Use what the enemy told you to hide away forever to help someone else go free. Teach everyone around you that "before" is a critical part of realizing what's already been done by God.

YOU'RE IN A FIGHT!

I'm not sure if you realize it, but you are in a contest for not just your immortal soul. You are in a fight for your purpose. If you think that it won't be a fight to get to your predestined position in this world, you are sadly mistaken. Even if you are reading this book and don't necessarily relate to the Christian faith, you are still created in the image of God. Each of us faces a lifelong battle with the devil. Yes. Lifelong!

Satan will never rest and watch us move into kingdom purpose. He can't stop it, but that doesn't mean he won't try to spoil what God is doing in your life. It is with the awareness of this information that we can begin to prepare for battle. Millennials, you must be ready to fight! Your generation is so gifted and brilliantly talented that you could confuse him. You don't have to be a scholar to use the Word against him. It's on you now to take the gospel farther than ever! It is your time to shine!

The devil knew you would have insecurity issues. He knew that depression would seek to wrap its arms around you to choke out your existence. He knew that the justice system would work injustice concerning you. He knew that bum of a man would abuse you. You may say, "Dre, if God knew it, why didn't He do something to prevent it?" I'm glad you asked me that question.

Before God ever formed you, He planned your deliverance. Before deliverance could ever deliver a delivery, He had a way of escape planned for you. Think about how you have made it through all the obstacles so far. And you are still here! You are still alive because it was already planned before time to be so. You are His instrument of praise. Your life demonstrates His meaning of deliverance, because your life speaks of His goodness and mercy following you.

Don't let battles beat you down. If something comes upon you threatening to destroy your family, your business, your progress, and ultimately your soul, fight! Put on the whole armor of God and resist what is standing against you. There is no valley that you can't be pulled from. There is no hole so deep that His arms can't reach you. There is no burden that cannot be lifted. There is no barrier that can't be broken down. If God knew and formed Jeremiah, He knows and formed you as well.

We don't have to be prophets to be cared for by the Master. Let Him take you to places that you have never dared imagine possible. It doesn't matter what part of the world you are in. God wants to bless you and use you for His purpose. Our weapons are not natural, but they are mighty because they pull down strongholds (2 Cor. 10:4). The moment I got a revelation that God appointed me to speak to people, my world forever changed. I began to value every minute of my life. I left behind my old ways of thinking to lay hold of a better mentality. I decided to rise above what I was taught about myself, what society told me, what enemies whispered and screamed, to become a better man.

Always remember that a calling isn't just about what we do publicly; it is more about what and who we are called to be privately that has the greatest impact. I'd rather be whole privately than whole publicly. So many leaders are broken privately and whole publicly. On our best days, we as leaders are still flawed, yet we possess the character and the mind of Christ to be projected for a generation to see. We cannot play around with identity.

We must be fully persuaded as leaders that God has already drawn up the plays, we just need to run them. Our world desperately needs men and women who are called by God to be whole behind the curtains. To practice holy principles where cell phones are not allowed. To make the ones nearest to us feel loved the most. This quality of life can only come by way of desire.

We must long for it, or it will not apprehend us. It will cry out in the streets for our attention, but never lunge itself into our arms (Prov. 8:3-11). Leaders, we must walk differently, think differently; the narrow path is to be trodden by our feet. Knowing who we are in Christ is the path that is the narrowest, and the most challenging to find. God will help us find it if we believe. This path helps us to be who we were destined to become. It is a necessity.

It gives me so much joy as a married father of two beautiful girls to know that God knows who we are! Discontentment can no longer rest inside of me because I know that God has allowed my life to take on shape. What fits remains, what doesn't fades away.

There is no shortage of hope when we live life knowing that God understands who we are. Every quirk, every temperament, every unique personality trait, all aligned to be used by the Holy One. Like one of my favorite worship leaders of all time Israel Houghton sings, "Everybody say, I am not forgotten. God knows my name!" I will praise Him because He knows my name! Hallelujah! He knows who you are!

chapter 10

THE TRANSITION OF TRANSFORMATION

"So built we the wall; and all the wall was joined together unto the half thereof: for the people had a mind to work."
—Nehemiah 4:6 KJV

2PAC WAS ONE of my favorite rappers growing up. When he died it felt like a family member passed away. I admired Pac's poetic mind and his generosity towards our community. He was a brilliant lyricist who is truly missed. One day as I was at home chillin' after partying with some friends, I put his tape (Yes, I said tape.) in a karaoke box that I kept in my room. I lay back listening to his song "Outlaw." In it he spoke of never missing an early grave. As I was singing along to the song, it got to the line about an early grave, and the tape slowed down. I heard "Noooooo" replace the music coming through the speakers as the tape was destroyed. I was afraid!

It was like something I watched in a movie. I chalked it up to a demonic influence. Years later, upon reflecting, I know fully that it was the voice of the Lord speaking from that box to shake me in my spirit. God wanted to transform me.

He had my full attention!

This event happened to me at an interesting time in my life. I was a recent high school graduate with the intentions of going to either college or trade school. I ended up at neither. Running the streets, chasing women, smoking weed and drinking alcohol was my lifestyle of choice. I was determined to live the thug life. Women admired the image, and friends encouraged it, but it was just that–an image.

This was a pivotal time for me because the trajectory of my life could have gone in several negative directions. I struggled with low self-esteem, depression, lust, and unhealthy emotions and passions. I was a mess who didn't know he was.

We tend to judge young people as if they don't have the capability to make decisions. Our society, in my opinion, babies young adults, thereby leaving them unaccountable for their actions. I wanted the lifestyle

I chose; I didn't want anyone to tell me differently. As I lived in a novel world with real gangsters and stronger temptations, I began to feel lost. I felt as if I was in over my head.

My friends became enablers, hecklers, and haters. I had a heart. Having a heart in the streets can get you killed. As I ran the streets of St. Louis, my friendly nature was immediately rejected. From women who were willing to have sex with me without any pickup lines, to gun-carrying goons, I experienced a rude awakening. This wasn't a world I was supposed to be in. I knew it, but I did not know where to turn.

VOCAL LESSONS

It was at this precarious place in my life that I began hearing the voice of the Lord. As a child, the church mothers taught me how to be patient to hear the voice of the Lord. These sessions felt more like vocal lessons looking back. I know that what we consider to be a vocal lesson is based on us making a sound, but vocal lessons–as they relate to God–occur when we tune our spiritual ears to hear what He has to say! The prayers of my grandparents kept me from being as delinquent as I desired. I was promiscuous but cautious, broken but knew where to get healed, hurt yet always helping others. Instead of dealing drugs, I worked. I found a job as an airport porter when I was 17. This job was cool because I got to meet celebrities.

Some were nice, and some, I'm still praying for. This provided another aspect of life for me that was important to see. The more I was around my favorite celebrated ones, the more it had me thinking that I could be like them one day. It was in this airport job that God again spoke to me. I mean, out of the blue, so to speak, I would receive a prompting in my heart that connected me to Him. He loves us where we are, not where we feel we should be. It was at this point in my young life that He met me with compassion and patience.

One day as I wiped down tables, the Lord said to me, "I'm preparing you for war." He also said to me, "I love you, but you have to leave this lifestyle behind. If you don't leave it behind, you will be destroyed." Each time He spoke it filled my eyes with tears and my heart with peace. The more He spoke, the more I listened. I had rebelled against His commandments. I wanted God but I still wanted to live my life the way I chose. My mother's lack of responsibility early on created independence in my heart. I relied on myself.

I depended on me. I knew what I would do. I could get the job done. Now I had an outside influence–God–wanting to get on the inside of me. I was scared. Back in the late 90s we didn't have fun at church like we do today. The guys I knew teased men who went to church. If you were young and a churchgoer, they ridiculed you. I mocked kids who went to church. It was lame to me. God was cool but church not so much.

Now here I was getting an earful from God. He wanted to change my life.

The devil was on me! "What will your family think? You will lose your friends. You won't have any fun. You will be poor. No girl wants a church boy!" On and on and on these thoughts bombarded my thinking. God pursued me relentlessly. I tried smoking Him away. I tried drinking Him away. Both to no avail. God gets what He wants; I just didn't know it at the time.

THE DECISION

The craziest sign that it was time for a change came from a thug I admired at school. This guy was a nightmare to his foes. He was a tough guy. One day I went to church with my grandmother, and I saw him there, although not the way I did when we went to school. In just a few short months he had completely turned his life around. I talked to him after the service. I was shocked beyond belief. He had cut off his braids, ditched the baggy pants, and exchanged his gangster image for a three-piece suit! It hit me like it would hit a person if Lil' Wayne cut off his dreads and removed his tattoos.

His transformation frightened me; I was shaking. I asked him why he changed his life. He simply said to me, "The Lord wanted to be in my life." His change-of-life statement rocked my world. Time was running out on the old me.

God was after my heart with no qualms about snatching me back from the dark side. Some of my friends and family teased me and offered no support. This time it was up to me to make the best choice I would ever make in my life. From the stopped Pac tape, to classmate conversions, to this inner voice growing louder and louder, I began to lose control of my normal. God had already warned me that I was on the verge of losing my soul. You don't hear much about this nowadays, that we can lose our souls trying to gain the world.

I had no intention of joining church; there were no desires of holiness in my heart. I wanted to be one of the best sinners ever! I thought I was tough; I wanted to live an ungodly life, but deep down I knew my grandparents had taught me better than that. With all that the Lord had brought me through in my younger years, you would think I'd bust down the doors of the local church to live happily ever after.

That's not how the story went for me. It took divine intervention. No man could take credit for my salvation. Not one!

TEAR DOWN TO BUILD UP

Our text deals with the life of the prophet Nehemiah. After hearing that the Jews were returning to Jerusalem after a time of exile, Nehemiah left his position in the palace as cup-bearer to the king in order to rebuild the once-strong Jerusalem. Nehemiah had a God-given desire to rebuild the city, but it would not come easy. Nehemiah is one of my favorite books of the Bible. Let me explain how it relates.

Jerusalem was once known as the place where God's presence dwelled. Due to her people's disobedience, God sought to teach Israel a lesson. King Solomon built such an impressive empire that many neighboring powers came to visit and see his kingdom (1Kings 10). It was this same empire that came crashing down due to its sin. It was this same empire that left an empty feeling in the heart of the prophet.

Even a cushy job in the Persian palace could not stop him from reminiscing on the good old days. I admire his ability to look back at what was and restore the lost glory. Nehemiah couldn't accomplish this on his own, and neither can we. Transformation is difficult to obtain. It's like everything aligns at once to stand against you.

Becoming who we are called to be is similar to reconstructing a once-luxurious temple. Sin rotted our structure and destroyed our walls. If we are ever going to get somewhere in our walk with God, we must tear down what's wrong in our lives by accepting the truth of God's word. When it's preached, we should strive to obey every anointed word to see our dreams and deliverance come to fruition.

I believe that's why preachers are attacked so greatly. We carry in our mouths the words of Jesus to set people free! If we do it right, we can help someone reach a place of transition. I met this place in my life at 20-years old. I had had enough of God compelling me to come; I was ready.

Before I gave my life to God, He and I had a serious conversation. I told God, "Okay, I will live for you, but I'm not going to stop getting high, and I'm not going to stop listening to my music. I'm not ready to live holy, but I'll live for you." Yep. That's what I said to the God of the universe. I'll never forget how simple His reply was to me. He said, "Okay, then you will be destroyed." It was the most straightforward truth I have ever heard in my life. It came from Truth.

His words prompted my transition. I finally did not want to let my wants, needs, and desires stand between me and my relationship with God. I didn't want my destiny cancelled or altered by my ways, so I changed my mind. I repented one night while high and drunk in my bathroom at home. I asked God to come into my heart. However, He nudged me beyond just a prayer of contrition.

God took me back to the old school that I remembered. He reminded me of those years in Sunday school and children's church when we waited on the Holy Ghost to fill our hearts by speaking in tongues. I stumbled into my room, got on my knees, opened my mouth and immediately I was in the Spirit. I felt His hand touch my left shoulder as I cried while speaking in tongues. When I got up from the experience, I was completely sober. I got up with zero desire for the vices I had held so tightly before. I was a new creation. I was born again! No more drunkenness, I was made whole.

To add to my experience, I got up with perfect English. My slang was gone. The desire for curse words was gone. It was my transition that transformed the course of my life. I was excited, but my family was skeptical. I believe my family was shocked to see the turnaround. I'll admit that it still took a while to accept holiness, but we all must grow in the grace and knowledge of who Jesus is (2 Pet. 3:18). The more I pursued God; the more He pursued me.

There were lots of changes that had to me made for me to walk this life the way it was meant. For me I had to leave a vast majority of my childhood friends behind. As the years have gone by, I've heard that most of them are either dead or incarcerated. I had to stop chasing girls to prepare to become a husband. Shortly after my conversion God let me know that He had someone special picked out for me, but I had to be obedient to get her. I threw away all my CDs and all my clothes and shoes; it was a total turn around for me.

Instead of frowning all the time, I smiled and laughed a lot. A burning desire to know more of the Bible was lit inside of me. I began reading book after book, learning more about the Christian life. I counted my steps when attending church before I was saved because I didn't want to go to church yet leave the same.

Now I had power to enjoy Sunday! I went back to the childhood church that my brother and I attended with our grandparents. The people were sweet and encouraged that God still saves. They also loved that I was so young with a desire to live for him. Young people, you don't have to be old to hear from God. Listen while you are the age you are so that you can be used the way He intended. I was on fire! I faced persecution as to be expected. Some family relationships became distant, other relationships superficial. I was determined not to go back to my old way of living.

This was my way out. This was my ticket to purpose! Instead of late-night parties, I studied. God told me to trust Him and never go a day without reading His Word. A commandment I still obey to this day. My transformation was radical. It was sudden yet progressive due to the amount of time God spent convincing me to become a better man.

It is my firm belief that God comes into a person's life to bring good news! He comes into our lives to give us eternal life; He comes also to make us better people. Since I had a leadership call on my life, He was hard on me. I could see things in the spirit realm. The devil wasn't too thrilled about this next dimension of myself.

SPIRITUAL WICKEDNESS

One night as I slept, I was attacked in the spirit by demons. These demons bound me up so I could not move and prevented me from speaking. As I was between realms, I heard their footsteps on the carpet. Then, they jumped inside my spirit. As soon as they jumped in, I had a vision of the cross. It was a gold cross like the one put on a necklace. Then I saw a grotesque hand grab the cross and enclose it with a fist. This dark force was unlike any I'd felt in my youth. It was much more sinister and powerful. It was trying to kill me!

The reason I know it to be true is the demons were preventing me from breathing. At one point during this attack, I managed to say "Jesus." Nothing else would come out. Just the name of Jesus. (It's all we really need.) When I released the name of Jesus from my lips the demons jumped back and fled.

Their goal during this attack was to keep me quiet. I could write another book on the many spiritual attacks I've faced over the years after conversion. Hell was mad! It lost a soul it thought it had. Plus, I was done being the tail. No more fear. I became fearless! Instead of swallowing my opinion, I blasted. I had to learn to use wisdom, but the switch was flipped with no point of return.

Once I was filled with the Holy Ghost, my eyes were opened to a whole new world. I began seeing spirits in people. I could feel demonic influences when I walked into places. I heard things in the spirit realm. Sometimes I would touch doorknobs or walls and feel a vibe. I also had dreams and visions throughout almost every day and night. My experience was far from just going to church on the weekend because Grandma said, "Get up, and go!" I was called, and I knew it.

I didn't always see or feel bad things. I could see the Holy Spirit living inside people. I could feel the power of God as they spoke. With this power came great responsibility that I had to yield my life to if I wanted to wield it. God made me a promise that if I walked in love, maintained my integrity, and took care of my future family, He would fulfill the vision in my life. I was excited to hear that I was going to be married. However, I did not walk in the Spirit consistently.

DIVINE CORRECTION TO CONNECTION

Hearing the voice of God is a practice that takes time. We can't be in a hurry if we want to hear from the Lord. We also must be flexible. He may begin speaking to you while you're brushing your teeth. He may talk in the middle of the night. He can use nature or movies or whatever else He sees fit to use to get us to listen. He also uses our mistakes.

Mistakes are an important part of the process. I almost made the biggest one of my life. I didn't understand as a 21-year-old that whenever God makes you a promise, it could take a while to receive it. I went on the hunt searching for a wife who was standing by His side the entire time. Let that sink in.

One day while at a friend's house we ordered pizza at a nearby pizza place. The girl who took my order had a pretty voice. We ended up striking up a conversation that led to a relationship. She was not the right one for me. She only wanted sex, and I refused because I wanted to live right. This girl with her tight clothes and arrogant attitude was all wrong for me. My family warned me, but I didn't listen. Her auntie hated me! To her I wasn't good enough. I didn't drive the latest model or make the most money. I ended up proposing to this woman, and she accepted.

Thanks be to God we ended up breaking up. I did not get my ring back, but I got my life back. My family was grateful, and I was an emotional wreck. Immaturity ran through my veins at a rapid pace. My problem was that I tried–in my own strength–to bring the vision God gave to me to pass. I walked in the flesh instead of the Spirit. I was led away by my own lusts and passions. I was so mad at God and myself. What did He do wrong? He had mercy on me.

If that girl and I had married, it would've ended in a divorce. She was fast, and I wanted to slow down. As we all must find a way to do when something tragic happens, we must move on. During this period in my life I was working at the airport. And even while I was dating this young lady, an unusual blessing was at my job right in front of my face. Her name was Llechor.

She has the oddest–yet intriguing–name I've ever heard. I used to always check the Burger King schedule to see if she was working. Ask her now, and she will tell you I "stalked" her. I'm not sure about that, but I was for sure interested in her. She was an attractive chocolate-skinned cutie with an elegance about herself. You'd think she came from a family of doctors and lawyers by the way she carried herself.

She was down to earth, and God was after her heart too. Somehow, some way I managed to get her phone number. We talked on the phone for hours. Having just come out of a failed relationship, I wanted to be upfront about my intentions. I told her I was looking to get married to someone one day soon, and I didn't play games. The first conversation we had on the phone was comfortable and natural.

She was 18 at the time; I was 22. Fresh out of high school for her, fresh into a new world with powers I didn't understand for me. I shared my faith with her in a balanced way; she spoke of her grandmother very highly and said she was a church woman. This for me was exciting! I told her when we went on our first date that I wanted to meet her grandmother.

The first time I met her grandmother I fell in love with her. She felt like family, which was weird since I'd never met her before. She told me some time later that when she met me the Lord said to her, "Now him I know." We had an instant connection. Llechor's grandmother and I talked on the phone and prayed together. She was a mentor to me. Funny enough, it was the relationship I had with her grandmother that made me aware Llechor was the person God wanted me to marry.

Looking back, it's crazy to think that the devil sent woman after woman to keep me from getting to my wife. Spiritual wickedness is real. Believe that!

SHE PLAYED HARD TO GET BUT IT WAS ALREADY DONE

I asked Llechor to marry me on February 10, 2001. I wanted to wait until Valentine's Day, but I didn't because I felt it was cheesy. Ask her, and she'll say it was due to the fact I couldn't wait. What confidence! Speaking of confidence, I basically told her we would be a great couple and example for the world to see concerning marriage. When I said this at work one day, she replied, "Who said we were going to be a couple?"

She played hard to get for a while. She said she was moving to Atlanta for school, and I was crushed. I didn't want to step in the path of her education. I knew what God had said but didn't want to approach her with a "The Lord said" line. I prayed on it, we dated, and I let God do the rest. I did stress to her that I wasn't going to marry a woman without her being filled with the Holy Ghost. I shared with her that if God did it for me, He would do it for her.

One night after work we prayed in my back seat, and she was filled with the Holy Ghost by speaking in tongues! To this day her life has never been the same.

I've watched this sweet girl from the projects of downtown St. Louis blossom into an incredible woman, wife, and mother. God has used my wife to transform me into a better person. September 15, 2001–the week of the most terrifying moment for our nation (9/11)– we exchanged vows and never looked back! When you set out to build a life with someone, there will always be attacks from the enemy.

Just as Nehemiah fought to rebuild the walls of Jerusalem, I was in a fight to rebuild the life God intended for me. Joining my life with this woman's was the fulfillment of a promise of transformation, but it was only just the beginning of things to come.

After much opposition, Nehemiah eventually rebuilt the walls of Jerusalem. God will never let man hinder His plans permanently. Rebuilding is a process already done in eternity. We must believe it, and walls will form! It is so!

chapter 11

DON'T ASSOCIATE ME WITH FAILURE!

"Plans fail for lack of counsel, but with many advisers they succeed." —Proverbs 15:22

REMEMBER GOING WITH my wife to a church years ago. Giving credit where it's due, an associate pastor shared a story with the congregation one Sunday morning. As Elder Bryant confidently stood in the pulpit, he glanced over the audience, paused, and spoke. The story was about a conversation between God and him. As they were talking, the pastor said to God, "God, I know that You can do anything but fail!" God replied to the elder, "Don't associate Me with failure." This response struck a chord in my heart. I didn't understand it then, but I feel I do more so now. Everything God does succeeds; nothing fails. That is a statement open to debate on a human level but not a heavenly one.

Heaven always makes the right choices; they're decisions made from an eternal viewpoint. God's divine plan streamlined into hearts full of faith can and will succeed. Elder Bryant's revelation led me to say to myself, "If God doesn't associate with failure, why should I?" A winner mentality sprouted from the seed of that message. It has blossomed into a strong cedar tree. If only it were as easy as speaking it once. It takes many years of failing to grow uncomfortable in the presence of it. Look at a professional sports team who has lost for decades; once they grab a taste of winning, the floodgates open.

I'd had enough of brokenness and sorrow; I wanted a higher quality of life. I made it my business to express to my wife when we were newlyweds the sort of life I wanted. I had witnessed up close for years my mom and other family members get the relationship game all wrong. I wanted to win. Failure wasn't and still isn't an option.

GROWING COMFORTS

When you set out to live the married life, there are some "growing comforts" that must take place for the relationship to survive. We hear much about the growing pains of life, but growing comforts for me are developments in the spiritual realm. I knew of marital stability from my grandparents' generation, so it wasn't a fairytale. But my wife and I came from adverse circumstances that came into our lives to keep us from becoming one flesh.

My wife by nature is tough. She's very sweet, loyal, and loving, but she does not play. One of the advantages of growing up black is it hardens you. We are simply used to a hard time. In order to withstand that sort of pain you must be strong-minded. I married my wife because she was beautiful and has the heart of a warrior. We naturally connected, but it took a while to see where each of us was coming from.

My wife early on never really expressed how she felt. I am the exact opposite; I speak my mind. This produces a conflict in relationships that challenges each spouse to study his or her partner.

God didn't create our differences for us to grow critical; He gave them to compliment the union. If we want comfort in our marriage, it takes growth; and growth takes time. What we sow we will reap if we do our part to nurture what we've planted. I wasn't satisfied with having a good marriage; I wanted a great one. I wanted a marriage that would go down in history as one of the greatest marriages ever. One of my reasons for wanting this was all the abuse I suffered as a child, all the roadblocks that prevented me from flourishing.

I'm a firm believer that when God brings His children out of great trials, it is so they receive great rewards.

If we lose a good job, a great one comes after it. If we lose an opportunity, it's because one comes behind it that is more significant. Trials come to bless us, not injure us. If we have the mindset that we are coming out the same way we went in, we waste our moment in the storm. Storms come to show us the leaks in our boats. Storms humble us and teach us a better alternative. Storms discipline us. Imagine sailors out at sea when the threat of a storm rises. They meet the challenge with experience and skill. Trials equip us to become more skillful in what we do.

One day while I was at work, my wife called me early in the morning crying. I told you already that my wife is super tough; when she cries, it's a big deal. We had only been in our marriage for a couple of years when this attack from the enemy happened. I'll never forget what I felt that morning.

She called and could barely get the words out, "DeAndre...!"

"What's wrong?" I asked.

"I woke up this morning and couldn't breathe; I managed to say the name of Jesus and the feeling went away."

"Are you serious?" I demanded.

"Yes!"

I was shocked that these demons were now messing with my beautiful bride. I was in a rage when I heard the news. I don't want to be attacked, especially while asleep. It's such a cowardly move of the enemy to attack while we cannot defend ourselves.

And, such is the nature of our adversary. He is a coward! I had had enough of him! It was bad enough that he attacked me as a child: immobilization with duct tape, beatings, molestation, and multiple attacks of sexual immorality. When I was water baptized after coming back to the Lord, I emphatically began screaming and shouting at the top of my lungs. I stomped out of that baptismal pool with great authority. For the first time in my life, I was free. I had no intention of going back!

As my wife shared this news with me, I felt power rise within me. Now I know it was the anointing, but then I couldn't describe it. I took authority over the devil in that moment. Instead of him binding, I was the one now doing the binding! In a turn of events, the failing one became the successful one! I commanded the devil to take his hands off my wife in the name of Jesus! He did! He has never bothered her in that capacity again.

We must be as bold as lions if we are to reclaim taken territory. We cannot afford to slink back to where we were before Calvary. Too many lives are at stake! If anything is pressing your life right now, attempting to drown everything you have ever worked for or what God has given you, you need to fight! My youngest daughter is very straight-forward. One day during dinner while eating homemade chicken noodle soup, my youngest looked up at me with the most adorable, fatigued eyes and said, "I'm tired of eating this." Get tired of failure!

Scripture deals with failure yet it also speaks of success. After many years of losing, I was determined to win. Not only did I want to win, I expected to win! I had the confidence and faith in God to thrive. I learned how to pray and intercede in my 20s. The desire fell to me from my grandparents and my ancestors. When our slave oppressors attempted to wipe us off the face of the earth, it was their fervency in prayer that gave them the victory. Somebody way before me knew the victory was already done! They heard about how Jehovah delivered the children of Israel from their oppressors (Ex. 14:30). They had read about Joshua and the Battle of Jericho (Josh. 6). They refused to accept failure as a permanent option.

They prayed until something happened! If we are to claim our rightful place, if we are to see our enemies annihilated, we must listen to the advice of the scriptures. Whether it's by way of reading it, hearing it preached, or listening to the word in the mouths of our friends, wholesome advice followed leads to a life of success. It's time for you to no longer give in to oppression. Leave depression behind. Come on! It's time to go. It may have ravished your emotions for decades, but now deliverance is here.

NEW FRIENDS

For many people, making new friends isn't something they want to do. Just the thought of putting one relationship to rest and starting again is work that makes them uncomfortable. Truth be told, most people would rather stay bound than to fight to get free. Influence has much to do with what direction we take in life. Me being a natural follower early on in life led to some bad associations that almost got me killed.

When my mom lost the townhouse, we ended up staying in a small apartment nearby my grandparents in St. Louis County. There I met a new friend. We hung out and turned up with the ladies, but it was an unhealthy friendship. One night he called me and said this girl he was dating had a friend. He asked me to come along, and I accepted. We went to a bad neighborhood where people were just hanging around. You could smell weed smoke from two blocks away! I'll never forget this night because it could've ended terribly.

My friend had a dope Pontiac Grand Prix. This car had lights underneath it with shiny rims and an enormous sound system. We pull up on the block with him blasting his music all down the street. I was upset because in my head I'm thinking, "With all these people out here, we're making ourselves a target." I'm telling you; my thought literally came to life. My friend was having trouble seeing the house numbers from the street. A dude came up with a bob haircut (That's a cool Afro.) and wearing a Michigan football jersey. He broke away from the crowd and leisurely walked up to the car.

My dumb "friend" rolled down the window and said, "Hey, can you help us find this address?"

The dude pulled out a 9mm and said, "Get the **** out the car, and if you move, I'm poppin' you!"

I came outside for this? I felt like Craig from *Friday*! I just wanted an off day. This was no laughing matter though. This man was serious. I had my hand on the door ready to run once he started shooting. I figured the angle of the gun would cause a bullet to hit me in the shoulder if he fired into the car.

My friend thought fast. He replied to the goon, "Huh?"

As soon as the guy began to speak again, my friend smacked the gun and drove off down the street at lightning speed! It was a miracle that he decided to drive in the direction of the crowd because the goon probably would have shot the car up. My friend drove frantically through main-intersection red lights, doing 80-100 mph.

He was yelling and screaming, "They tried to jack me; they tried to kill us!"

As traumatic as the experience was, I found myself trying to calm him down. I wanted to get home safely. It would have been insane to avoid getting shot only to crash. We were both filled with adrenaline but made it home safely.

After this incident I feel like my friend's life took a downward spiral. Shortly before this night, he had shot and killed his father for beating his mother. A history of abuse came to a head one day in their garage. He told me that he confronted his father for yet again laying hands on his mother. An argument ensued with the father lunging at my friend with a hammer. My friend told me he had no choice but to shoot his own father in the head as an act of self-defense. I felt so bad as he was investigated heavily by local law enforcement. To go through that and now face a loaded 9mm Glock in the face made him snap. God was with us that night, and I am grateful He was.

The reason that thug couldn't shoot us, the reason we never got hit driving through all those red lights, and the reason I wasn't anywhere close to his house the day he killed his father was because my destiny was already set by God before the world began!

That may sound arrogant and boastful; I say it is truthful. We've all heard stories like this that end fatally. God looked backwards in my life with future Dre looking forward and stopped the enemy. God protected me from becoming a sex offender. He protected me from becoming an out-of-wedlock father, and He kept me from a premature death! I can truly say that nothing can keep God from loving me (Rom. 8:35-39)! God has destroyed everything that has tried to sentence me to a life of failure.

I am beyond thankful for His hand on my life. The moment I was saved, it was there I made a vow to never waver in my faith. I feel if I can do it, so can you. When we surround ourselves with the right people, we hear the right information, and that leads to making the right decisions. I was tired of having losing seasons. I was tired of feeling purposeless. I grew exhausted lying about my age to fit in with the older crowd, trying to blend. I was done with that. I was done with hurting people. I wanted a new life. He gave me one.

I'm just a kid from St. Louis with big dreams. I am a person who practiced hearing God's voice at an early age. I am a work in progress. What I am not is a failure. You're no failure either. We all have days and moments that we wish we could erase. We can't, and it really doesn't matter now. I know a Man who will do the same for you that He did for me. He will lift you out of the deepest, darkest, most horrible pits life can devise.

Plans are good only if they are nurtured with wholesome advice. It doesn't matter what ethnicity you are; failure can get a permanent grip on all of us if we are not careful. There are many who feel successful because of their earthly accomplishments, yet they are bankrupt in the court of eternity. It's better to be poor in time while rich in eternity as my pastor used to say. Don't get to the highest of heights only to realize your feet never left ground zero.

Please don't spend your best years following the worst advice. Make every effort to see your plans carried out to the fullest measure. Always remember all things are possible with God (Mark 9:23). I hope that you find the courage to break away from unhealthy influences, so you can become all of what you were meant to be.

With all that I have I encourage you to find a way to break free. Leaving the familiar is the hardest thing I've ever done, but it's also landed me in the softest hands. I know of none other who can love, lead, and serve like Jesus. Every day I just shake my head wondering why God chose to be so merciful to me.

He erased the shame of my past, to use me as a witness to new beginnings and power. Today you may walk in weakness, choose to leave it behind for power. Your pain can be turned into something far greater than what caused it. Please let my life serve as an example that Jesus is no respecter of persons (Acts 10:34). I believe with all my heart that He will help any heart that receives His love. He will break any curse that's been pronounced over a life.

He will bind up the wounds and pains of the broken-hearted to bring healing. Our God is a deliverer. He knows how to release us from what could potentially destroy us forever. Satan fights us with bills, financial pressures, insecurities, etc., to try to get us to believe in a false image of ourselves. If we accept what he says, we will never become who God created us to be.

If you want deliverance, I want you to pray this prayer with me:

"God, I come to you weak in my flesh but believing that with you all things are possible. I thank you for keeping me through adverse situations filled with anxiety and pain. I now realize that it is not Your will for my life to be lived depressed. It is not Your will for me to accept failure and defeat. With Your grace, I ask right now that you heal my brokenness. I take my depression, I take my suicidal thoughts, I take my aggression, I take my acceptance of failure, I take my mediocrity, I take my fear, and I nail it all on the Cross where sin's penalty was paid for me. I'll watch it hang there until it dies. Whom Your Son set free is free indeed. Grant me now, Father, success in all my life. Bless me to be a blessing. I love You. It is so!"

Prayers mixed with faith give lasting results. Thank you for agreeing with me as we seek your deliverance! Don't associate with failure any longer.

chapter 12

HUNGER GAMES

Alpha, Omega, Ruler of Eternity, Bright and Morning Star,

The Spirit that burns in me, River Opener,

Light of the golden city, Sin Eraser,

Your blood voids the penalty, Emmanuel, Son of God,

Son of Man, Messiah, Jesus exalted,

You're Lord and we must admire, Root and Offspring of David,

Your goodness we taste it.

—"I Exalt Thee" (Dre Williams)

A DESIRE TO TASTE is a symptom of hunger. The *Hunger Games* trilogy is a deep concept. In it lies life and death, rich and poor, strong and weak, victory and defeat. Watching each of these movies left a lasting impression in my mind. Life is like this trilogy–full of heroes and villains. I'm not into stereotyping either, but I do notice traits in people.

My country–America–is one of the wealthiest countries in the world. From French fries to filet mignon, if you can afford either extreme, my country has it. With all the resources we have as a nation, we probably have the highest hunger problem in the world. I'll explain. To hunger means to have a deep, unfulfilled desire. It means to have a yearning. It can be as innocent as a craving or as vicious as starvation.

Hunger at any level results from a lack of nutrition. In our cities and in our communities (rich and poor alike), people face some sort of want. My thought deals with spiritual hunger. Our country may be founded on Christian principles, yet our nation is not a theocracy. We are not a people united after the heart of Jesus. Our history is messy and toxic. At the time of this book, our nation is divided more than I've ever seen in my lifetime.

We hold various beliefs and opinions. Churches remain divided on Sundays, and we seem to be content to keep it that way. I played Hungry Hippo as a kid. Though it was fun, the hectic dog-eat-dog nature of the game makes a good analogy. The hustle and bustle of life leaves us scrambling to reach the top. We pull down any and all that seem to be making more progress than we are. Hunger leads to irrational choices that can produce bitter consequences. Our fragile states of mind mixed with complex ways of living make hunger the top, unfulfilled priority in many people's lives.

We owe it to ourselves; we owe it to God to seek a better solution. I'm so glad God allowed my spiritual stomach to growl as a teenager. The inner promptings and nudging took my spirit from inquiry to necessity. I simply had to know why I suffered so much at an age I couldn't defend or protect myself. I was desperate. I wanted answers. I fought against being swallowed up in bitterness; I fought against rage. There was no earthly sustenance that could fill my starved soul.

What about you, friend? Have you felt that craving for something you knew that you needed yet couldn't find? I'll spare you the cheesy "Come to Jesus" speech that we've read many times before in books. I'll also refrain from scaring you in to salvation. I stand behind Jesus as Savior. Period. I won't change my position. I share that I once was hungry. He fed me to the point of satisfaction! If He did it for me, He will do it for you.

FILLED, NOW HUNGRY

Soul security satisfies the eternal requirement, yet our purpose still needs establishing on earth if we are to live in our calling. It is possible to be saved yet hungry in a different way. Once our salvation is fixed, we must move on to maturity (2 Peter 3:18). We start out as infants in the things of the Spirit; we must progress from our state of infancy. One of the ways we mature is by growing in our gifts. God uses unusual methods to cultivate our gifts.

One of my gifts is public speaking. I shared previously how music has played a huge role in my life. I also shared how God told me to use rap as a way of reaching young people. I had it planned in my mind how things would go; for the most part, it went that way for years. I would get invited to rap on Fridays at my local church then other opportunities presented themselves with friends. My life took an unforeseen change in the winter of 2008.

Up until then, my wife and I attended black churches. It wasn't even a thought to visit other places. It was what I was used to. I love my white brothers and sisters, so no shade. I just never considered it. One of my cousins invited my family to a church in the outer suburbs of STL for a Thanksgiving Eve service. It was a predominately white congregation. I immediately recognized the cultural differences within this church. At the time, where I was from, men could not wear hats in church. Our ushers were trained on sight to punch anyone in the mouth who crossed the church's threshold wearing one. (I'm kidding! Relax.)

We could not eat inside the sanctuary. Women were forbidden to wear pants or make-up. I hated the treatment of newly-converted saints. Church was awful and awesome at the same time. It was a place where the Spirit freed men and women from sin, yet men bound the same people with legalism and tradition. It began to wear on me so much I thought it was time for a change. This church–the one my cousin invited us to–became our new church home.

At the time, I loved the freedom and energy I felt when we first attended. It was a fresh start, a different experience. It took a while to adjust to a different style of worship. I believe it also took the pastors and leaders awhile to get used to us. We were a young black family that wanted to serve. St. Louis is a divided city, but I felt a hunger to meet and minister to people who were different than I was. It was in this church that my gifts began to grow. I started out volunteering as an usher. It was far from what I felt God was calling me to, yet I loved the brotherhood of the ushers.

Their love is what really won me over. I didn't care if they ever recognized me as a preacher or a teacher. God gave me a hunger for community, a hunger for fellowship. I loved it. My wife ended up serving in a position I felt was more meant for me. She became a sound/media person. With my background in musical production, I figured God would use me there, but He had other plans.

I'm not sure if I was a good usher or not; I just wanted to serve. Each Saturday night you could find me at the back of the church with my arms raised and a smile on my face. As time went on, and my wife and I made friends, I had opportunities to either act silly on stage or do short video announcements. I'll never forget the night they prayed us in as new members. I fell out when one of the leaders laid hands on me.

At that moment, I knew this was the place where God wanted me to be. My grandmother did not like our decision to leave the familiar to step into the unknown. I felt deep in my heart that she was being protective of me. And, because I love her heart, I assured her that I had truly heard from God.

THE PRAYER THAT SHOOK THE CHURCH

A couple of years went by, and little by little we adapted to our new surroundings. Most of the whites were sweet to us while others were afraid. I never tucked in my blackness to fit in. When you're black and try to fit into a culture not meant for you, it's awkward. I'm not sure if we were ever truly accepted, yet I do know God used them to help us develop as leaders.

One Saturday night during worship, the service was laid back, but the Spirit was moving powerfully. It was my night to usher, so there I was posted in the back as usual. One of the assistant pastors was preaching that night and began to pray in tongues. The power of God was strong, and the service took an unusual turn. It led to more worship.

Suddenly the pastor had words in English to say. He said to us, "As I was praying, I saw a person in the Spirit praying to God. You are called, and you know you are called. You don't have your grandma's calling or your grandpa's. You are called by God. This person was putting prayers in a bottle and throwing them in the ocean like you see in the movies. But this person had filled up the sea with their prayers. You're just throwing them out there–over and over–asking God when He's going to answer your prayers."

At this point something ignited in my spirit. I felt like he was speaking directly to me. It locked me in one place to where I could not move. As he continued speaking to the crowd, he said, "The person I saw in the vision was Dre."

I was floored! It felt like the word was explaining my situation. For years as a child I had prayed, and prayed, and prayed some more for a better life. I had begged God to become a better person. At 12, I had longed to be used by God. At 20, I had felt I was ready to run off and preach to a lost world. I had found my passion; I was ready to go! Or was I?

When I first got saved, Christian bookstores were sprinkled throughout many cities. I had an intense hunger to learn the Word of God. One day a pastor friend I worked with and I were at one of the stores. We came across a pastor's wife who was the clerk. My friend introduced me to her and when he did, she started prophesying to me.

"Young man, stay faithful to the Lord because He's about to take you through some things to show you who He is. How will you know He's a Healer if you never get sick? How will you know He's a Provider if you never need provision?"

I didn't even understand what provision was at the time, let alone grasp what it meant to walk through a valley. Her words scared me. It was a new world for me. Deep inside there was a confirmation that let me know she was telling the truth. Fast-forward nine years. Here I was ushering in a predominantly white church, receiving another accurate prophecy from the Lord.

"Is he here tonight? Is his wife here too? Grab her!" said this powerful leader.

The man of God had us come down to the front to be prayed for. It was so exciting. I remember saying to myself, "I'm not crazy! God really did promise a bright future! We are on our way!"

We left the service on a complete high. The preacher asked God to remove the wall that kept us from our purpose. We had a promise! A promise holds you over until the word is manifested in your life. Things remained the same for a while after the prayer, so much so that I began to question if this man truly heard from the Lord. We can get foolish and doubtful when we don't see things right away. God was moving but not nearly as fast as I wanted Him to move. I'm convinced–no matter what–that prayer works and prophecies are true. We must wait for what He has decided for us, not what we have constructed in our minds.

PREACHING RAPPER

If you had told me years ago that my desire to rap and freestyle would be used at a predominantly white church and not at a place I was familiar with, I would not have believed you. Don't get me wrong. I believe God moves in unexpected places, but when He wants to do it in your life, that makes it different. Little by little, God began preparing me for stage life. My first stint at church was singing background vocals for one of the worship teams. Opportunities to lead were few and far between. It didn't matter to me, though. Making music is my passion, so I loved it.

The worship leader would let us come to the studio to work on tracks for each set. This was perfect for me. My hunger began to intensify because God was taking me higher! I served this way for a couple of years until another worship leader took over. We instantly hit it off, and I became part of that worship leader's team. One Tuesday night during prayer and worship, I was joking around with one of the young adults who was a PK (preacher's kid).

She said, "Dre, I think it would be awesome if you rapped!"

My first mix tape was listened to by the worship community. Don't ever feel like your music can't open doors for you, even if they aren't as big as you'd imagined.

I reluctantly agreed.

"What will these white people think?" I laughingly whispered to myself.

The time came for the set, and our worship leader that night was cool and let me rap! My wife was out in the audience knitting, and when she heard me rapping, her head popped up! It was a simple moment that led to many more opportunities. I could not believe I was in the outer suburbs spitting bars! As my confidence in this new way of ministering grew, the prophetic began taking over my lyrics on stage.

One night when I was on one of the senior pastor's teams, I freestyled something that went like this: "Father, we're so patient. Father, we're so waiting. Divide the waters for Your sons and daughters, lower the mountains, fill up the valleys, do it in a hurry because You're so worthy."

The co-pastor looked at me, stunned. I was also. This was a move of God. It didn't stop there. God began rapping through me as well. He said: "Son, I'm so worthy, and yes, I'm so faithful, pouring out My glory on those who're thirsty. I lower mountains and fill up valleys. I'll do it in a hurry because I'm so worthy."

The crowd was shocked! I have way too many stories like this to share in one chapter. The one who grew up feeling like an orphan, the one who was betrayed. The one who was least likely to be used to impact ordinary people in a profound way. This was a God moment, and I took it seriously.

Looking back, I'm grateful God used me in that capacity. I went on to remix the old hymn "I Exalt Thee." It's a crowd favorite. I performed that song so much that I grew tired of hearing it. But every time I rapped to it, worship was released and lives were changed. A simple rap to an old-time favorite was used to refresh a multigenerational people. Wow! Only God.

You may ask, "What was the rap?" It was so simple. I remember my oldest daughter wanting to play at the time. I was ready to write. I don't like lots of activity when I write. When I managed to break away, I wrote this:

Alpha, Omega, Ruler of Eternity,
Bright and Morning Star,
The Spirit that burns in me,
River Opener,
Light of the golden city,
Sin Eraser,
Your blood voids the penalty,
Emmanuel, Son of God,
Son of Man, Messiah, Jesus exalted,
You're Lord and we must admire,
Root and Offspring of David,
Your goodness we taste it.

The idea popped into my head to use a song that was familiar to introduce rap to an age group that felt it was taboo. This challenge was conquered as elderly white women waved their fists in the air screaming my lyrics. Thank God for the talented people around me who helped bring out such an amazing song. I've heard several stories of hearts touched radically. One man told me after one Sunday service that as I was rapping, one of his son's friends was singing the lyrics and was filled with the Holy Ghost!

I gave and give God the glory! It is crazy to think the years I wrote and performed to walls and small audiences ended up bringing me before great people. This one song that never was released on radio or with a label changed my life and thousands of others. The rapper was released because God already had it in mind to release him in a unique moment and way! The prayer I prayed in my car years ago was superseded by the will of God! Isn't God good? My hunger for music led me to thousands of hungry souls. Hunger plus hunger equals power and victory!

THE BEST IS YET TO COME

One book cannot contain what God has done in my life. I wanted you to see that God raises up ordinary people to do miraculous works. The musical opportunities in St. Louis led to ministry opportunities. I've served in a store-front church, and I've served in large churches. At the time of this book, I have relocated to Dallas, TX. I'm so excited to see where my God uses my talents next. Dre the student turned into a preacher who then turned into a rapper who turned into a leader who became an author. The little abused boy has grown into a full-grown man.

The once insecure, bashful child screamed in the ears of Haitian prisoners that Jesus is Lord and God!! The one bound by sin now preaches deliverance to all who would hear. Just like me, the best days are yet to come! I don't believe any of us have seen how good God can be. His love too transcendent to be measured. His abilities too numerous to count. His blood too precious to taint. I live today in a place God prepared before time.

I live today in a mercy that was new before newness. I stand in a liberty before freedom, and a compassion before consequences. Every day I live my life blessed because I am alive. God could have let me die as a child, then as a teen, and even as a man, but He hasn't. It is with tears in my eyes as I write that I can say vulnerability has reached the tough-minded kid from STL. Every day is valuable to me because it's one I didn't have to see.

I have a lovely wife of 18 years who I've seen beat major giants in her life as well. I am a man today who has everything I need, and I thank God I do. My hunger to live for God has been satisfied. My hunger to push beyond my past was satisfied with divine independence. With the help of the Lord, I broke free from religious barriers and moved into who He called me to be. I have so much more room to improve and grow.

You and I have only scratched the surface of our potential. Be hungry. Be satisfied. It's that simple. Jesus said, "Blessed are they which do hunger and thirst after righteousness: for they shall be filled" (Matt. 5:6 KJV). The word "shall," simply put, is covenant language. It is binding and cannot be reversed. Your last cannot overshadow His shall. Your doubts and fears cannot compete with a shall! If He wants you, He gets you. Game over. He wins every time!

Don't ever forget that God is before us always, perfectly aligning our destinies with planned escapes from that which would destroy us. With a faith like this, we cannot be stopped! Your life. My life. Our lives have so much hope and expectation. A purpose and a future that are irrevocable! Because, as it pertains to the mind of God, It's already done!

CONCLUSION

I AM CONVINCED THAT God knows where we are in any and all phases of life. No matter what the devil threw at me as a child, I still progressed. That is an indictment against the power Satan possesses. All along it was God who worked in me for His good pleasure (Phil. 2:13). Our experiences should never make us feel as if our futures are threatened. The lessons we learn along the way help prepare us for the futures we daydream about. We are all in this together! Please don't allow yourself to become isolated due to a season of testing. Get with strong believers who will help you look to God always. Even as our world moves faster and faster each day, God's pace will never be altered by His creation. Trust Him to see you through the dark places of life. His work in our lives has already been preordained in His masterful wisdom. My conclusion to you is simple. Do you believe it?

ACKNOWLEDGEMENTS

Lord Jesus, You deserve all the glory! You are my very best friend! Thank You!

I want to thank my mother, Nedrita Williams, for not aborting me. Your bravery is respected. To my amazing wife, Llechor Williams, your support and friendship have meant so much to me. I love you and appreciate your spirit in my life. To my brainiac children Lauren and DeYanni Williams. DeYanni I am honored to parent a special child such as yourself. Never stop dreaming. Never stop doing good and what is right. To my Lolo, you are a sharp arrow in the hand of the Lord. Let Him use you, Baby. To my grandparents, Charlie and Mary Williams, thank you for taking me to church as a child.

Lively Stone Church of God will always be my first church home, and I want to thank my grandparents, Earnest and Ruth Greenlee, for instilling Jesus' love and principles in my heart. RIP to my father, Delbert Greenlee, from whose cloth I was cut. Your time on earth was limited, but your impact is far-reaching. To my siblings Montez Morrison, Tamara Scott, Lynn Brown, Tyrell and Javon Greenlee. My love for each of you is forever! To my uncle Tonio Williams, thanks for showing me what it means to be a man. To my uncle Charles Williams who beat me up as a kid, your tough love made me tough. To my auntie Toi, your whippings made me cry. I love you, Auntie, thank you for all your love! To my auntie Dena, who always picked me up and took me back home. To my auntie Wendy, I love you! To my stepmom that I call "Madre" now, Naomi Greenlee. God mended our relationship, and I am grateful.

To the late Bishop James "Al" Johnson, you are an incredible inspiration to me. Your messages made me a man of integrity and honor. To Pastor Ron Stephens, your Sunday school classes on marriage challenged me to be a husband every day! To the late Sister Heavens, your encouragement early on in my walk gave me confidence. To Evangelist Donna, who was encouraged by my walk with the Lord. To the late Prophetess Evelyn Moore, I miss you. My wife misses you. Thank you for speaking into our lives. Your leadership is legendary.

To Pastors Jim and Jessica, we had some great moments. Thank you for letting God use you. To Pastors Mark and Tina, thank you for the times we served together. To Pastor Ron, we loved God's people together!

To my auntie Angel, your friendship and love are deeply appreciated.

To Emmanuel and Harriet, thank you for modeling Jesus with excellence; I salute you. To Calvin and Latrice, for loving on us and sharing your wisdom and friendship. To David and Leslie, for your unwavering confidence in my family and me. To Elayna Etuk, for your kindness and creativity. To Gloria, for being used of the Lord to open international ministry to us. To my friends in Haiti, we love you! To my new pastor Bishop T.D. Jakes, First Lady Serita Jakes, and the entire Potter's House, your love I have felt already!

To my good friend Olu, for teaching me to branch out. To all my relatives and friends that I did not mention, please forgive me. I love each of you! To all the ministers of the gospel of Jesus Christ who paved the way, laid down your lives, denied your flesh, and promoted holiness, you mean more to me than you will ever know! To every author I have ever read, to every songwriter whose songs I've ever sung, I say thank you. To my ancestors who sacrificed and dealt with racial prejudice, terrorism, and injustice, I honor your legacy. And finally, to my precious readers, thank you for going back with me to where it all started. We laughed, cried, and met God during it all. Your support is such a blessing. I love you!

HOW TO BE SAVED

WITH ALL THE OPINIONS on how to be saved, I can only share with you what has worked for me. According to chapter 3 of the book of John, Jesus told Nicodemus that in order to enter heaven we must be born of the water (baptism) and of the Spirit (infilling of the Holy Ghost). If I were you, I would listen to the apostle Peter who told the multiethnic crowd on the day of Pentecost to repent, be baptized in the name of Jesus, and be filled with the Holy Ghost by speaking in tongues. Turn from your lifestyle that falls short of biblical standards to a living God. Regardless of how you may disagree, it's the only saving strategy that sustains. Please find a church with this belief and walk with God until the day you meet Him face to face! Be blessed!

LET'S STAY CONNECTED!

I would love to hear from you and pray for you! If this book has impacted you, please email me at:
dredreemer@gmail.com

For speaking engagement opportunities (serious inquires only), email:
dredreemer@gmail.com

Follow me on:
Instagram @dre_will
Twitter @lifeofdre
Facebook @drewill
YouTube @LifeofDre

For more on my ministry and musical journey, please visit:
dre-williams.com

For all donations:
paypal.me/DeAndre646

MY TOP BOOK RECOMMENDATIONS

1. *Destiny* by T.D Jakes
2. *The Name of Jesus as Immanuel* by Bishop James A. Johnson
3. *The Oneness of God* by David K. Bernard
4. *30 Minutes to Raise the Dead* by Bill Bennett
5. *You Have It in You* by Pastor Sheryl Brady
6. *God is Going To Make You Laugh* by Bishop Noel Jones
7. *The Love Revolution* by Joyce Meyer
8. *Praying Through the Promises of God* by Bishop Nicholas Duncan-Williams
9. *Post Traumatic Slave Syndrome* by Dr. Joy Degruy